Mirror Explorations

By Peggy McLean

> * Symmetry
> * Mirror Math
> * Spatial Puzzles

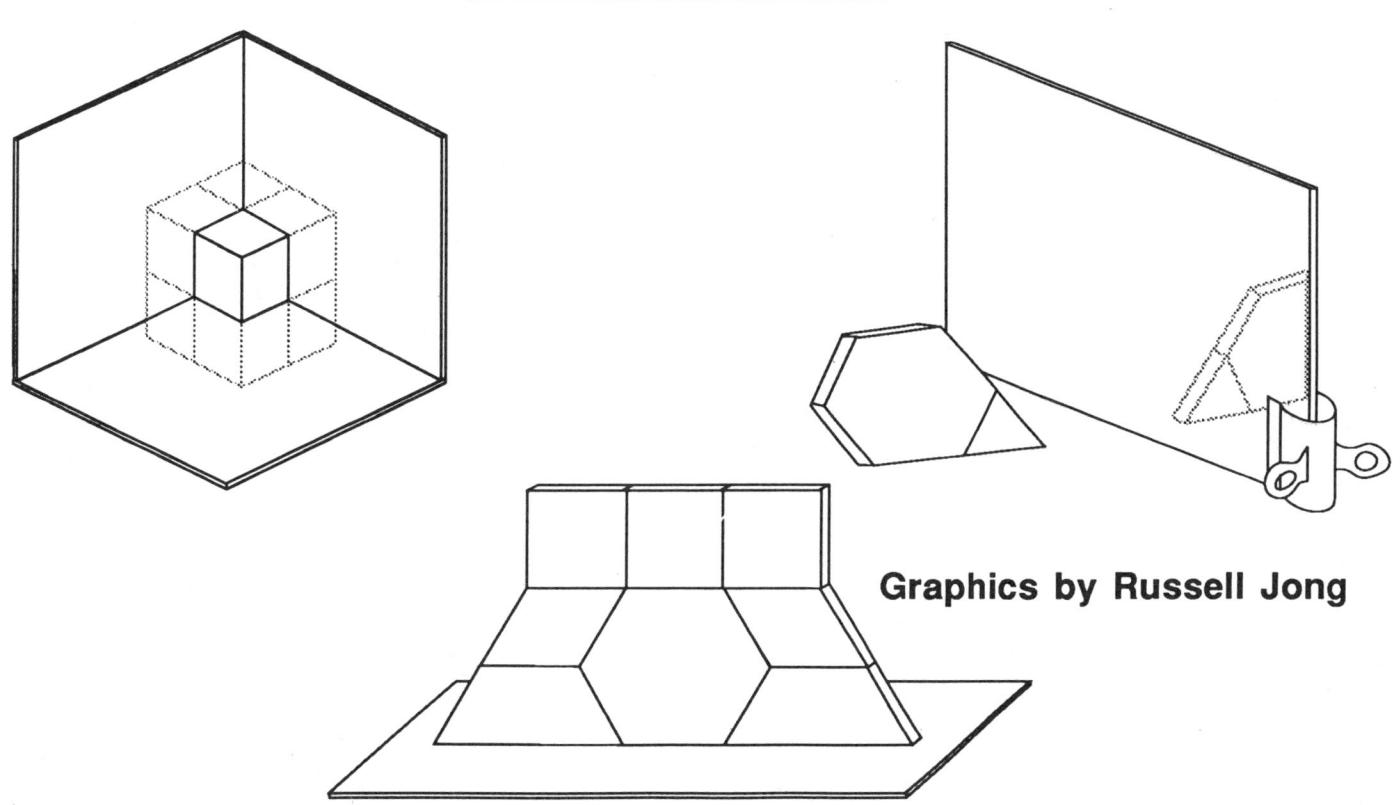

Graphics by Russell Jong

ACTIVITY RESOURCES CO., INC.

A mirror is a powerful educational tool as well as a source of wonderful imaginative play. You might even find yourself trying to push or pull images with the mirror until you experience what can and can't be done!

Mirror Explorations is a collection of challenging activities using manipulative materials, mirrors, Reflecta® and/or Mira® to develop concepts of symmetry in elementary mathematics. The book includes the operations of counting, addition, multiplication and division. Mirror picture puzzles, crossword puzzles and construction puzzles test the student's understanding of symmetry.

This book is lovingly dedicated to my husband Dan.
—Peggy McLean

Permission is given to individual teachers to reproduce any part of this book for classroom use. All other reproduction rights remain with the publisher.

Copyright© 1993
Activity Resources Company Inc.
P.O. Box 4875
Hayward, CA 94540

EXPLORATIONS

Place a mirror flat on a table or floor.

The larger the mirror the better.

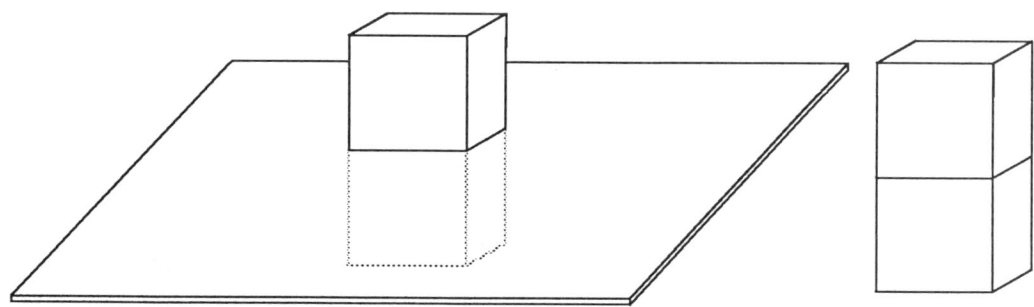

Put one block on top. Next to the mirror, build what you see.

Add another block! Move it around and build what you see.

Sketch

1.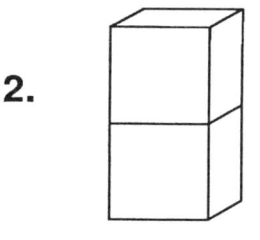

2.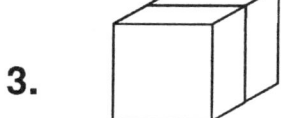

3.

Block Challenges

**Build each shape. Put one on the mirror.
Can you build it next to the mirror?
Guess first. Circle Yes or No.
Now try to build it.**

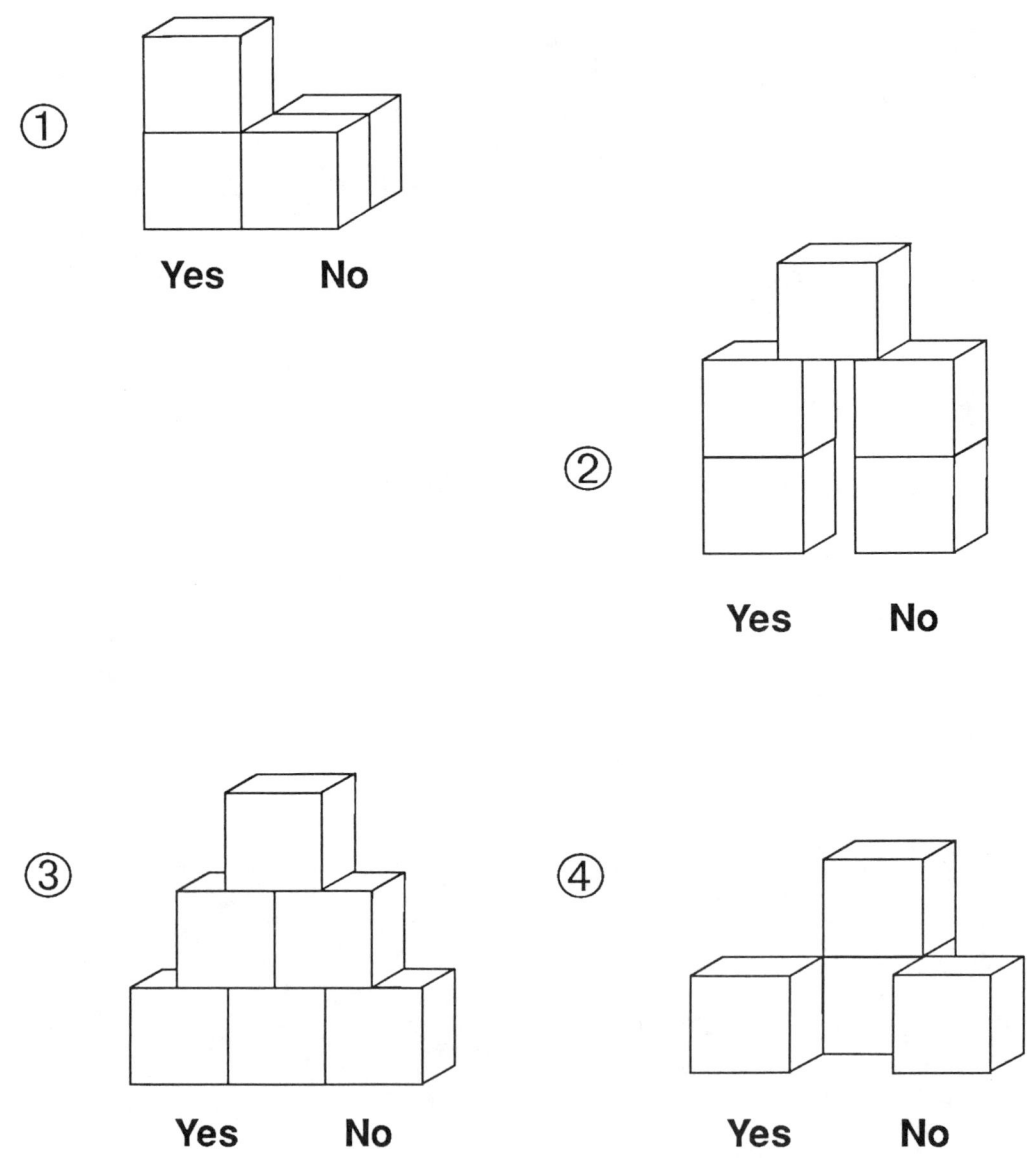

① Yes   No

② Yes   No

③ Yes   No

④ Yes   No

Build some for your friends to try!

Pattern Blocks

**Build each shape. Put one on the mirror.
Can you build it next to the mirror?
Guess first. Circle Yes or No.
Now try to build it.**

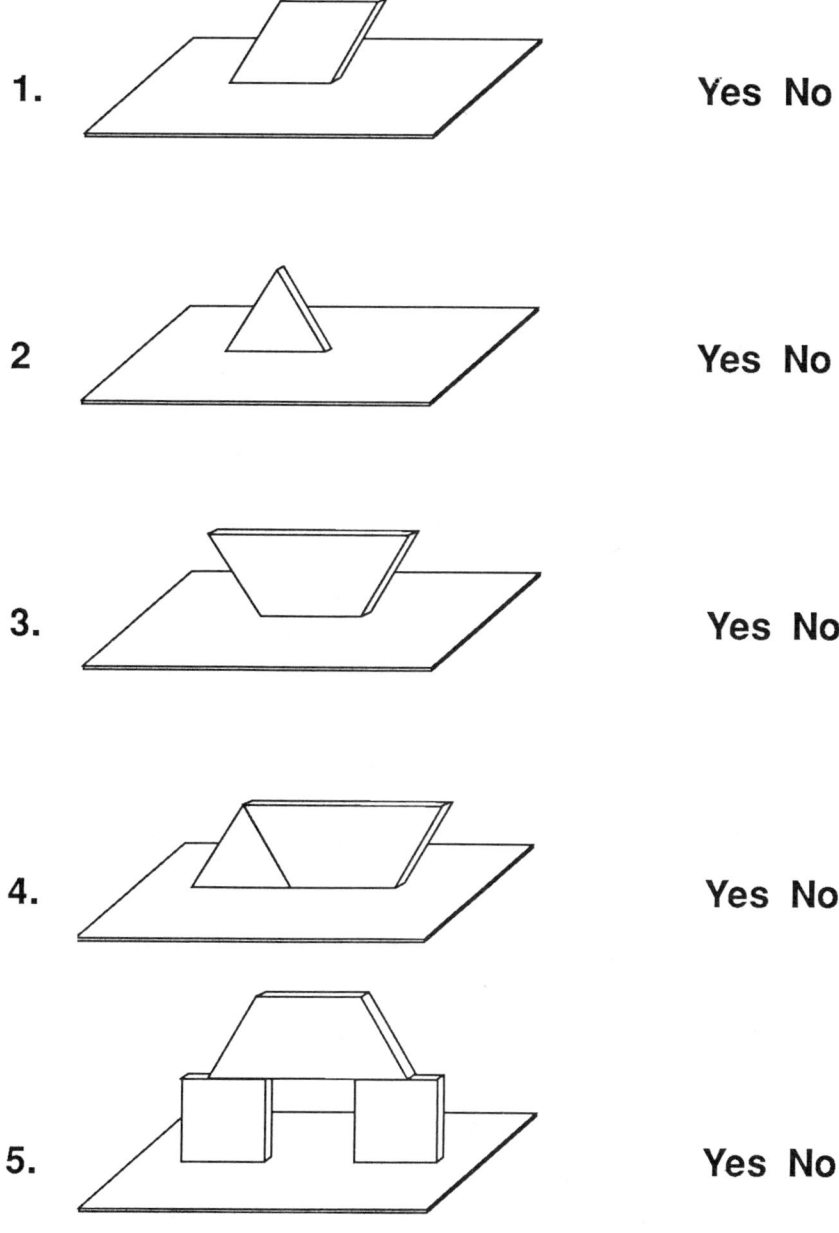

1. Yes No

2. Yes No

3. Yes No

4. Yes No

5. Yes No

Pattern Block Challenges

Circle Yes or No.

① **Yes   No**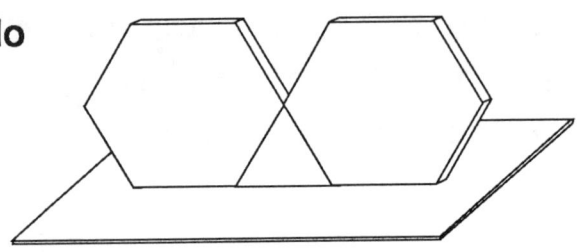

② **Yes   No**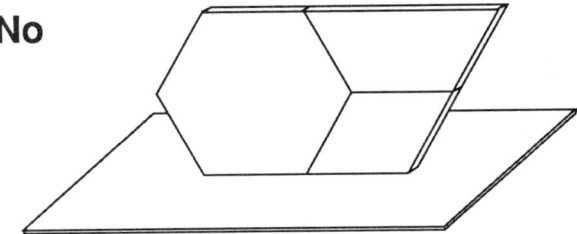

③ **Yes   No**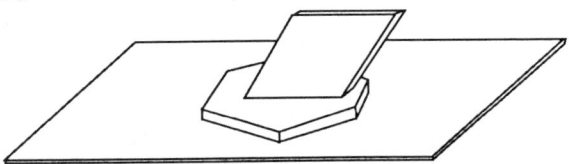

④ **Yes   No**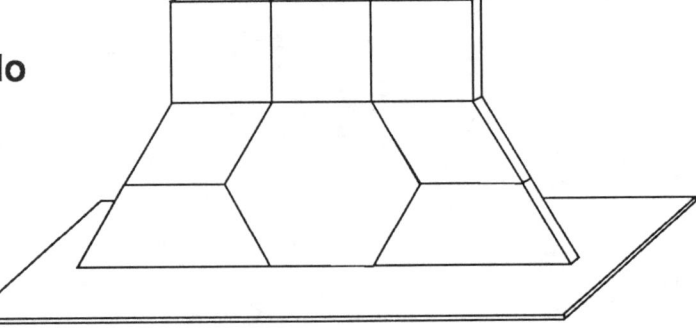

Pattern Block Challenges

⑤ **Yes   No**

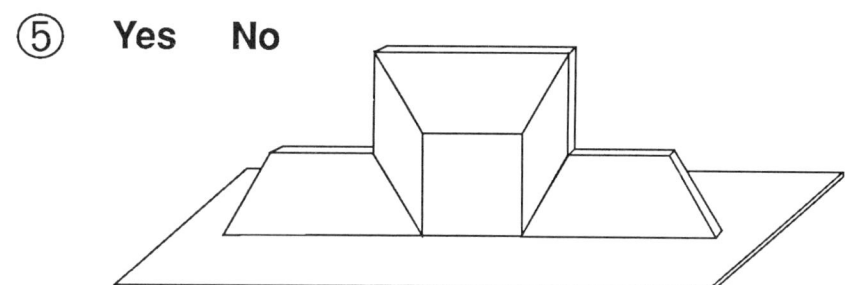

⑥ **Yes   No**

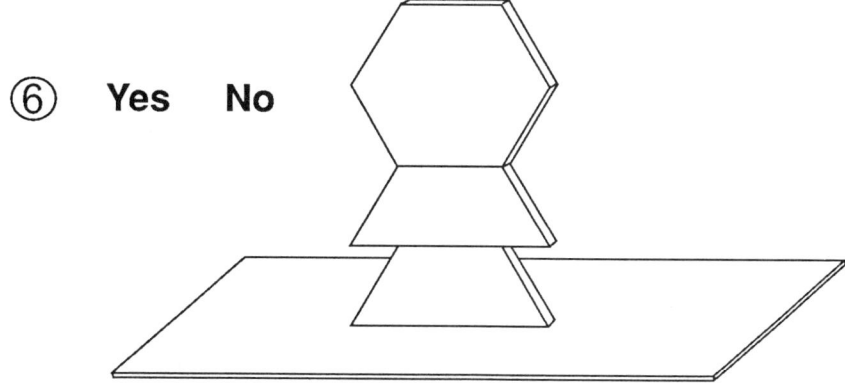

⑦ **Yes   No**

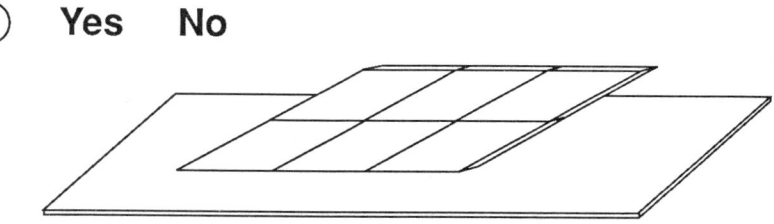

⑧ **Yes   No**

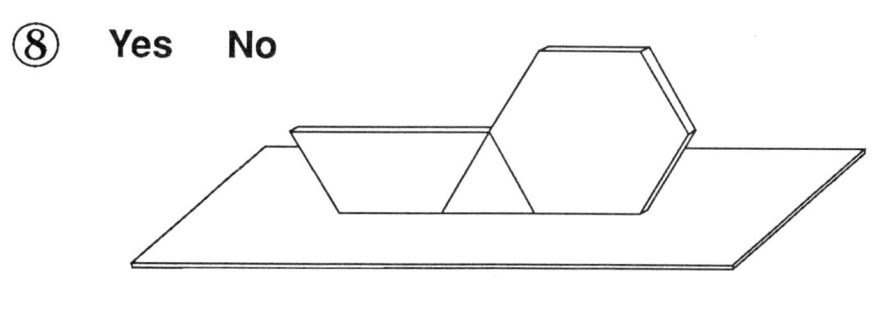

Make up your own!

Rods

**Build each shape. Put one on the mirror.
Can you build it next to the mirror?
Guess first. Circle Yes or No.
Now try to build it.**

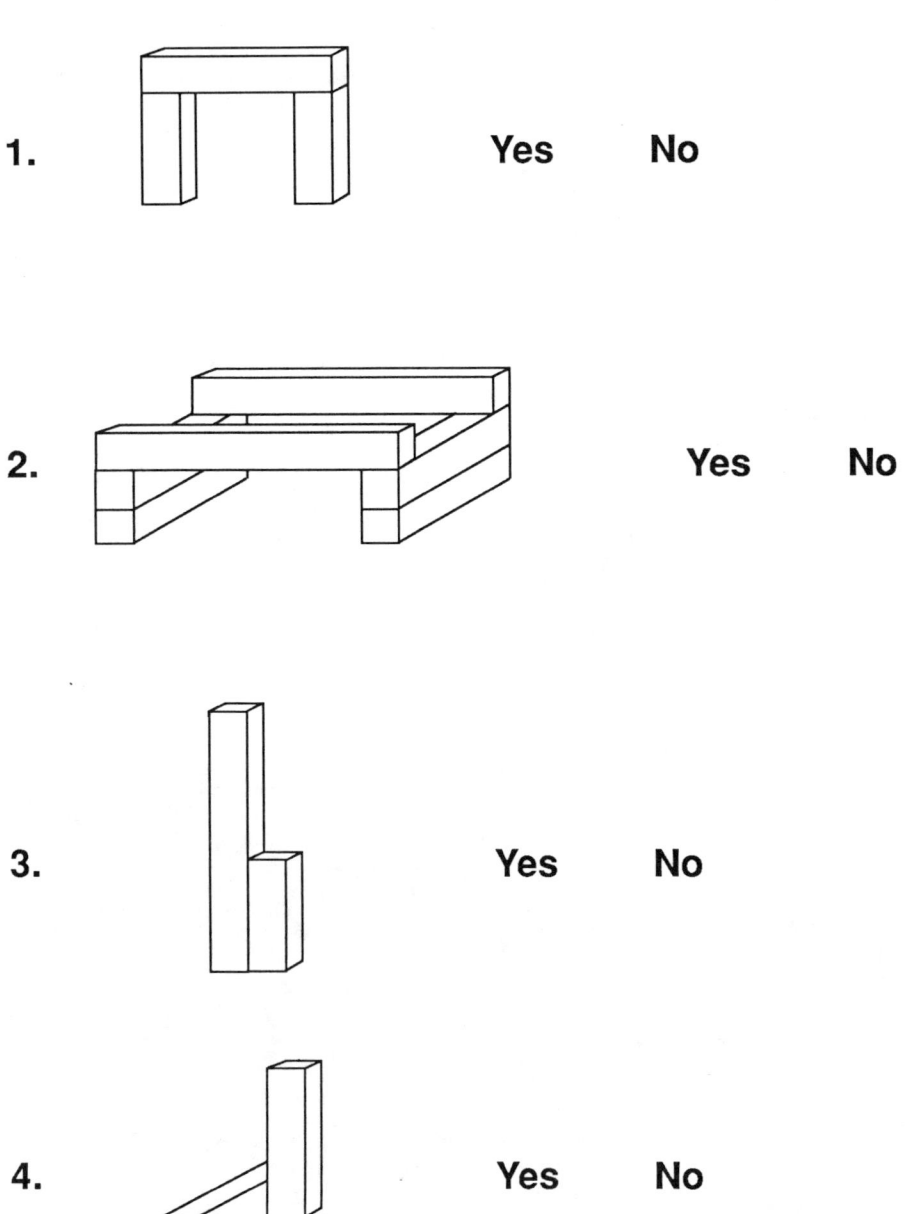

1. Yes   No

2. Yes   No

3. Yes   No

4. Yes   No

Rod Challenges

Circle Yes or No.

1. 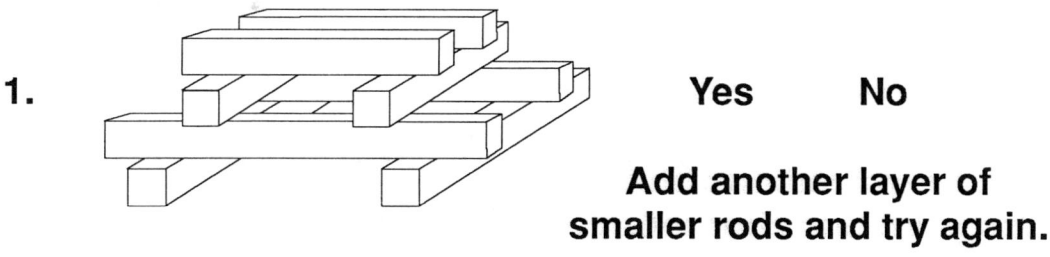 Yes   No

   Add another layer of smaller rods and try again.

2. 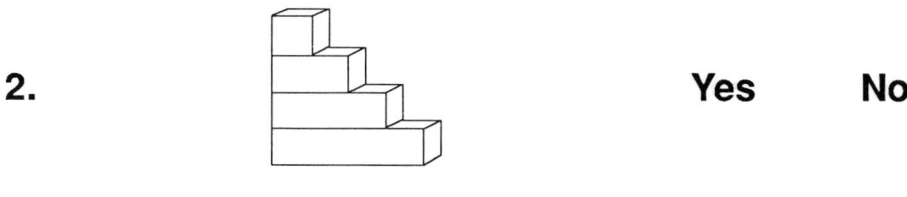 Yes   No

3. 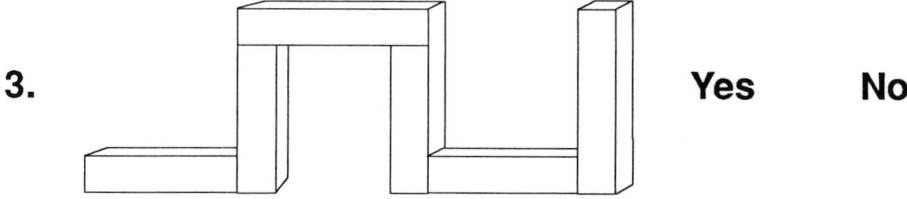 Yes   No

4. 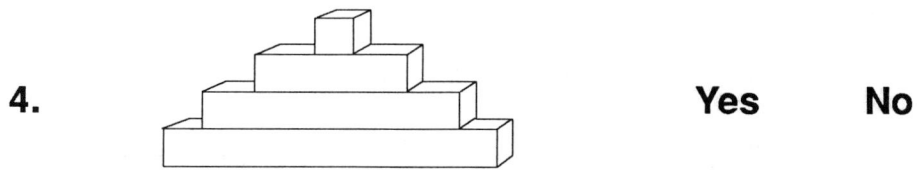 Yes   No

Make up your own!

EXPLORATIONS

**Stand your mirror on one edge.
Use a giant clip or clothespin to hold it.**

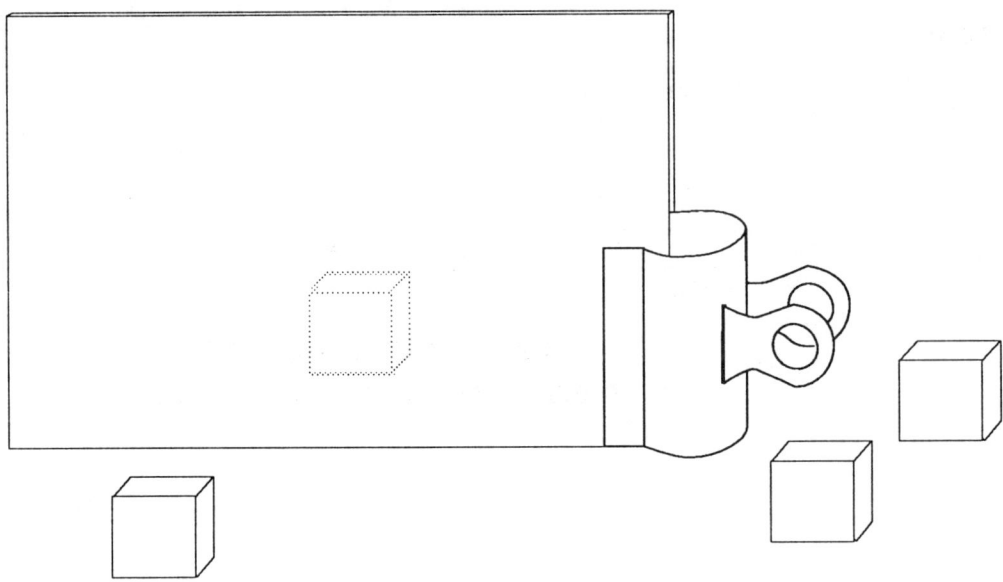

**Get some cubes. Put a cube in front of the mirror.
Next to the mirror, build what you see.**

OR

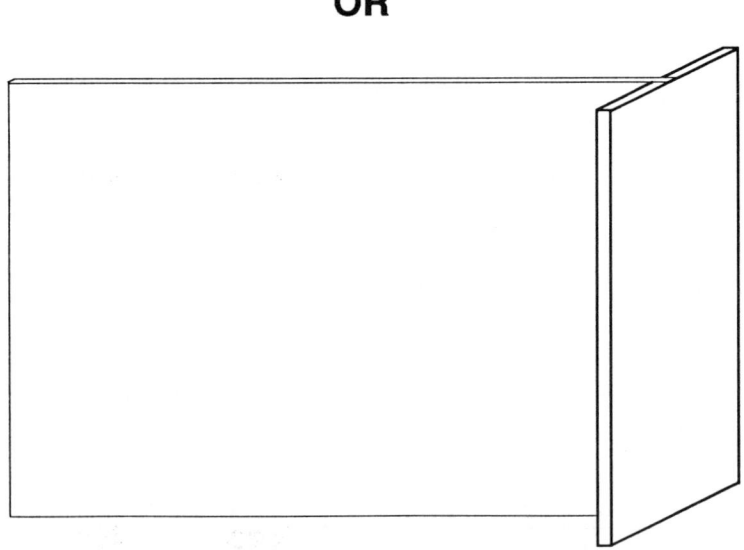

If you have a Reflecta® or Mira® (transparent mirror), match the reflection by building behind the mirror exactly what you see in the mirror.

What did you discover? Go back and build some of the structures that you put on TOP of your mirror.

Mirror Recording Sheet

Get your favorite building materials.
Build a design in front of the mirror.

Match the reflection by building behind the mirror exactly what you see in the mirror.

What I put in front of the mirror.   What I saw and built.

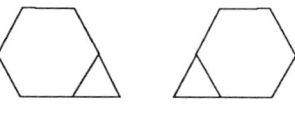

Discovery:

When you put something in front of the mirror . . .

Pattern Block Reflections

**Draw a line on a large piece of paper.
Put your mirror on the line.**

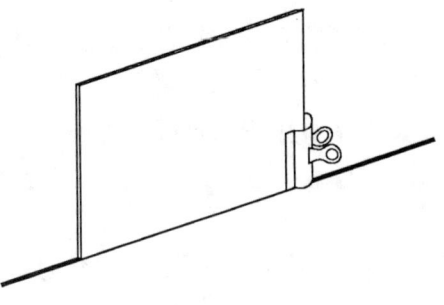

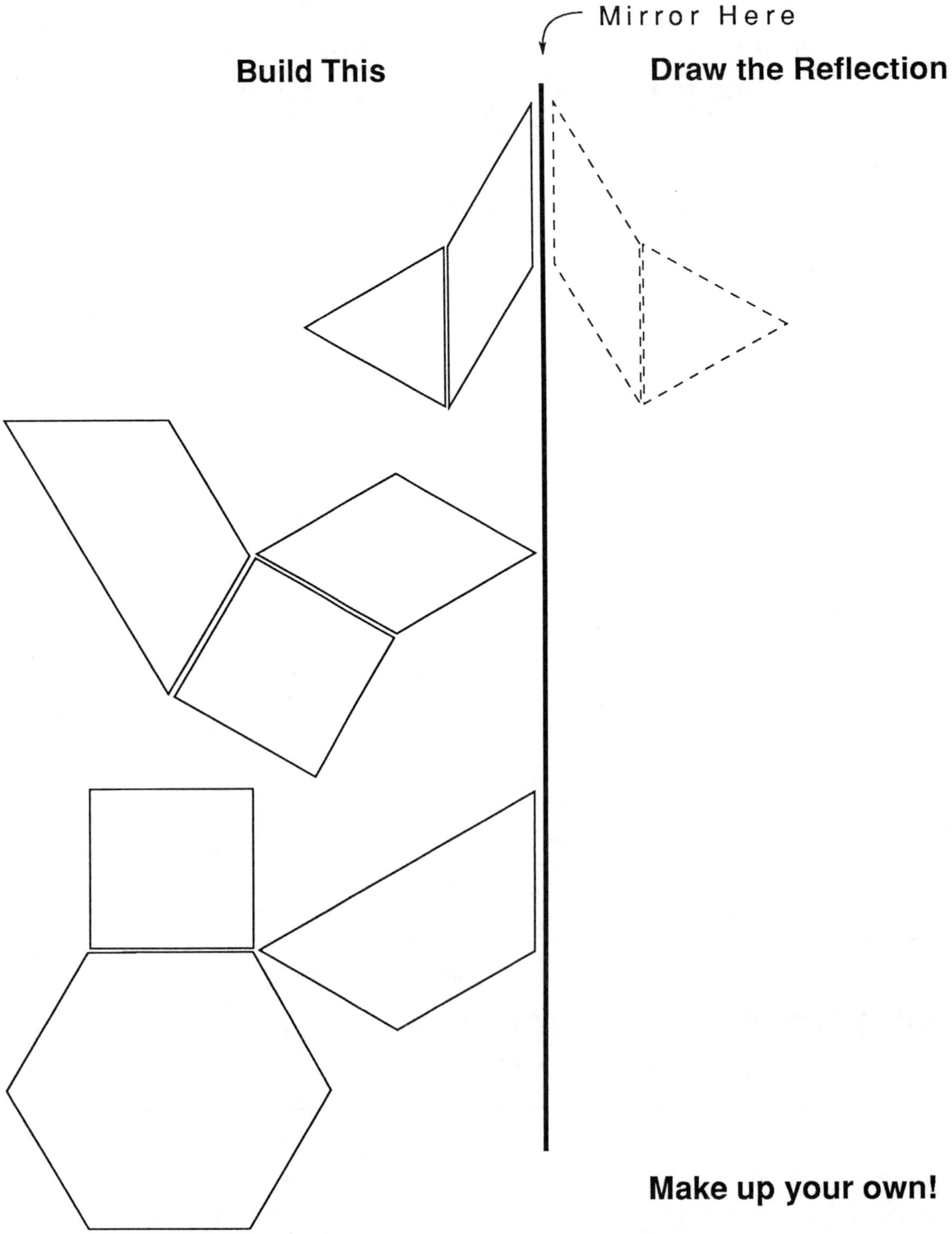

Mirror Here

Build This **Draw the Reflection**

Make up your own!

Pattern Block Challenges

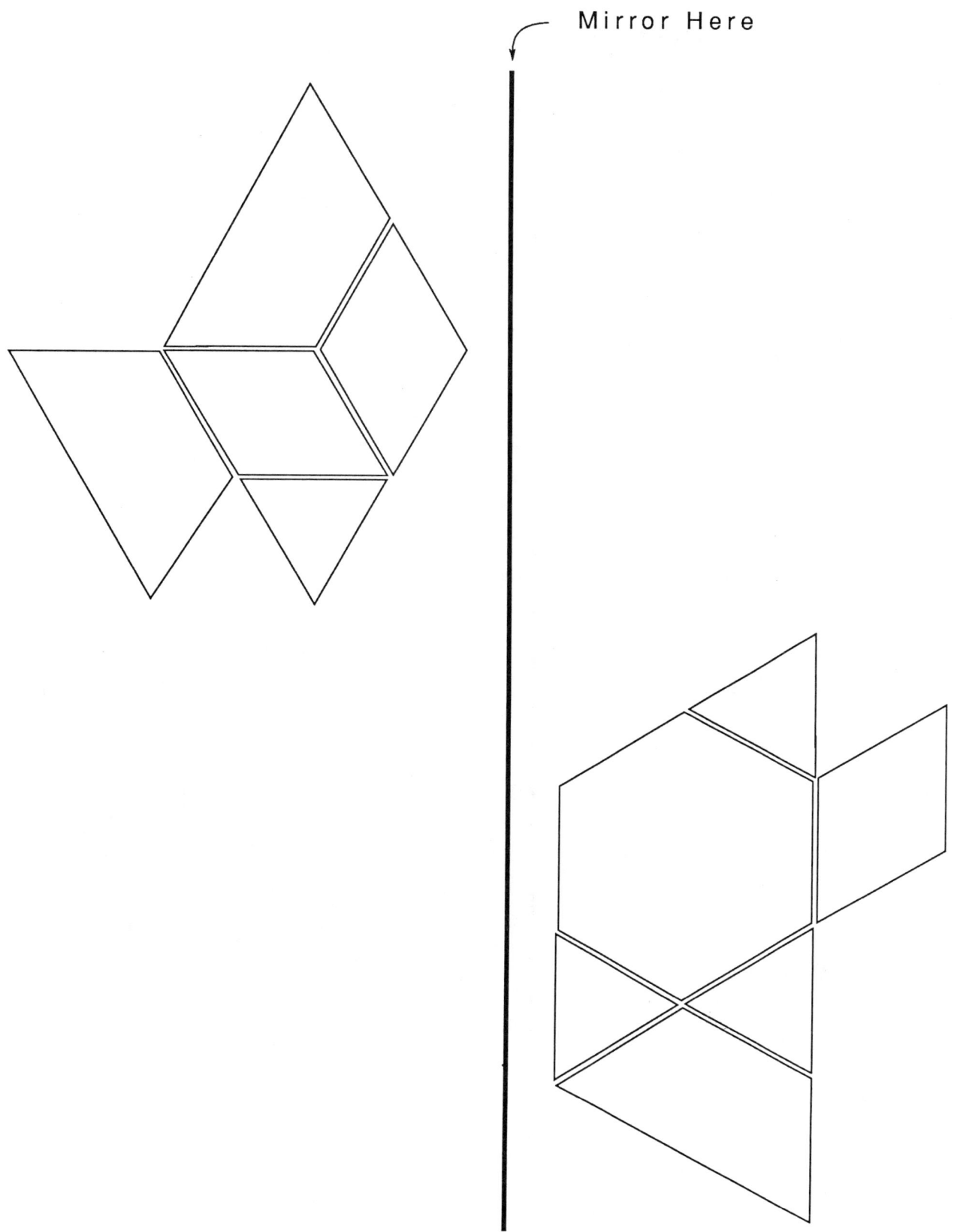

Mirror Here

Make up larger puzzles!

Rod Reflections

**Draw a line on a large piece of paper.
Put your mirror on the line.**

Build   **Draw the Reflection**

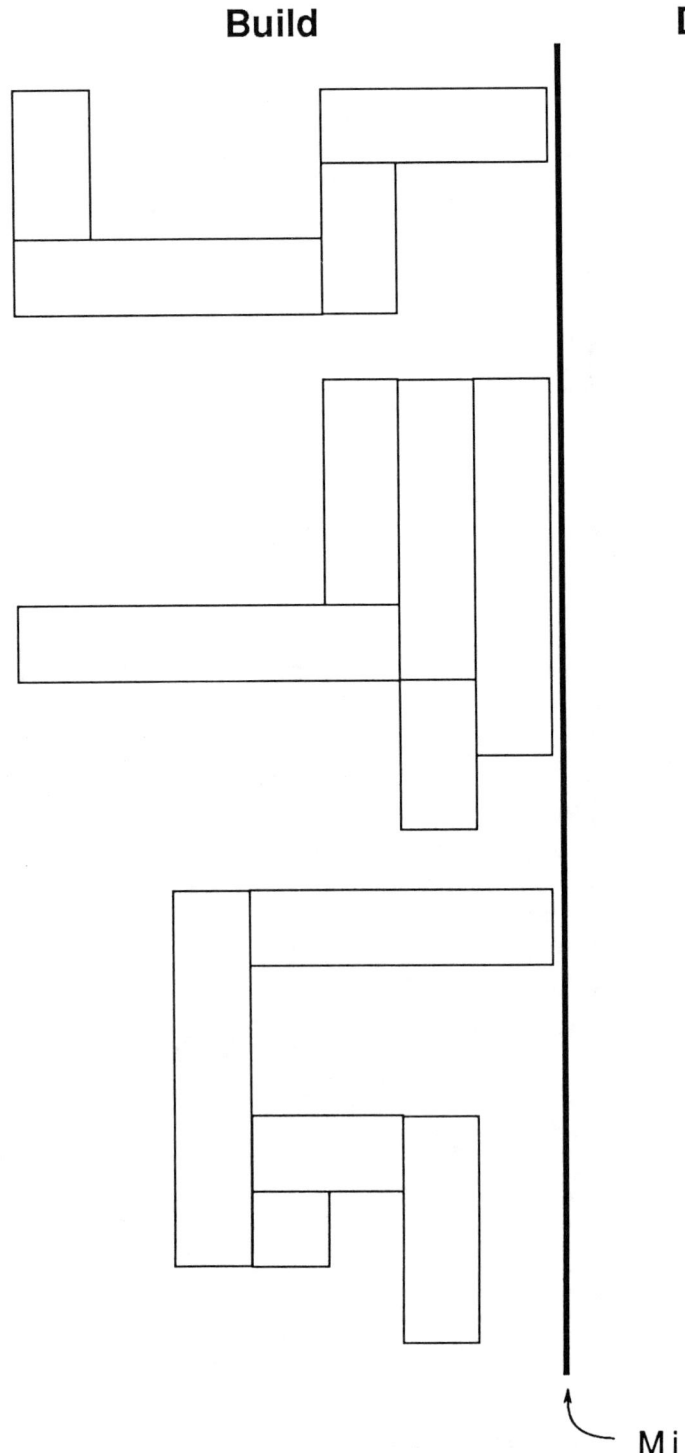

Mirror Here

Rod Challenges

Mirror Here

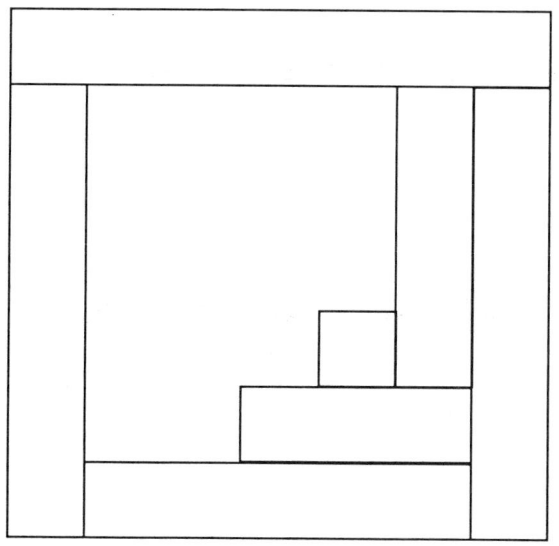

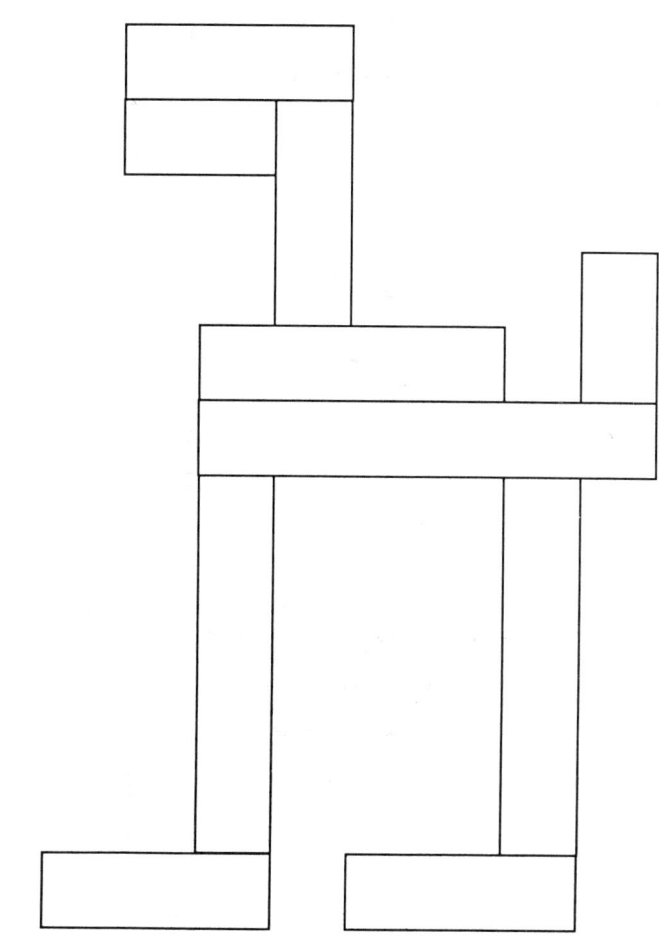

MIRROR MATH

Addition

Put your mirror on the line. Write the math problem that you see!

1.  $\underline{\ 4\ } + \underline{\ 4\ } = 8$

2. 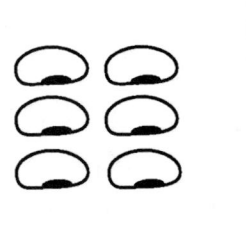 $\underline{\ \ \ } + \underline{\ \ \ } =$

3. 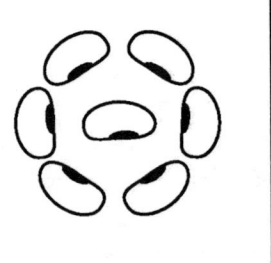 $\underline{\ \ \ } + \underline{\ \ \ } =$

4.  $\underline{\ \ \ } + \underline{\ \ \ } =$

Make up your own!

Addition Challenges

Put your mirror on the line. Write the math problem that you see.

1.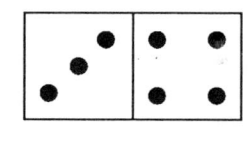

   $\underline{3} + \underline{4} + \underline{} + \underline{} = \underline{}$

2.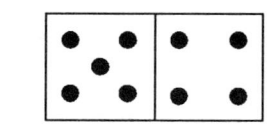

   $\underline{} + \underline{} + \underline{} + \underline{} = \underline{}$

3.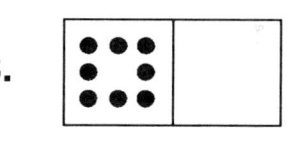

   $\underline{} + \underline{} + \underline{} + \underline{} = \underline{}$

You can make problems with larger numbers like this.

Use this side as tens place.   Use this side as ones place.

4.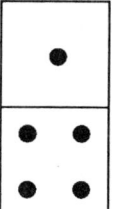

```
    1 1
  + 4 4
  ─────
```

5.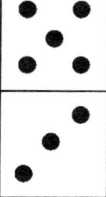

```
  +
  ─────
```

6.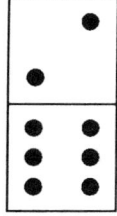

```
  +
  ─────
```

Addition Challenges

Multilink

①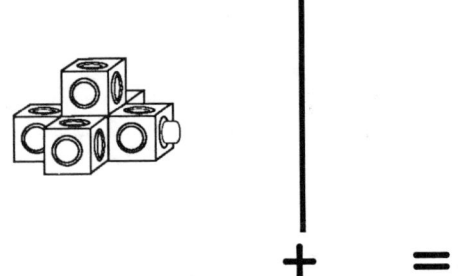

___ + ___ = ___

②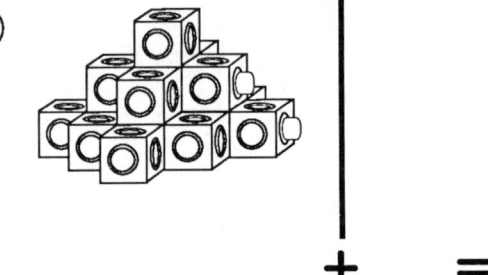

___ + ___ = ___

③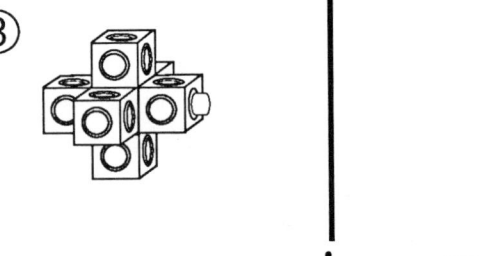

___ + ___ = ___

④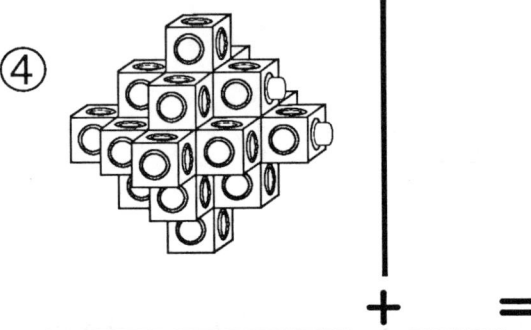

___ + ___ = ___

Rods

⑤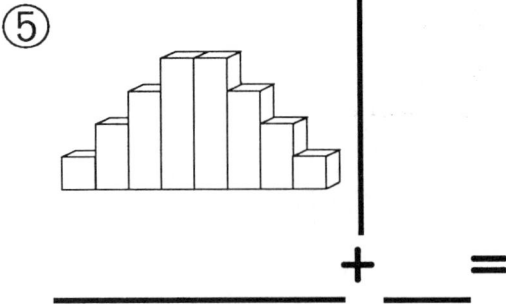

___ + ___ = ___

⑥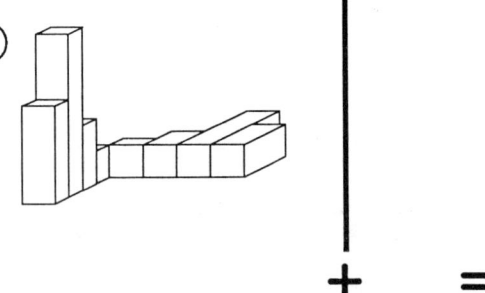

___ + ___ = ___

⑦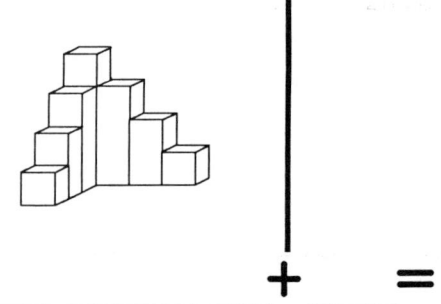

___ + ___ = ___

⑧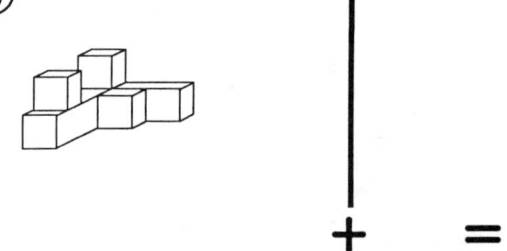

___ + ___ = ___

Mirror Math
Invent Your Own

Build and sketch each problem. Write the problem and answer.

1.

2.

3.

TWO MIRROR EXPLORATIONS

Use two mirrors. Place them on the dark lines.

Build and record what you see.

What did you discover?

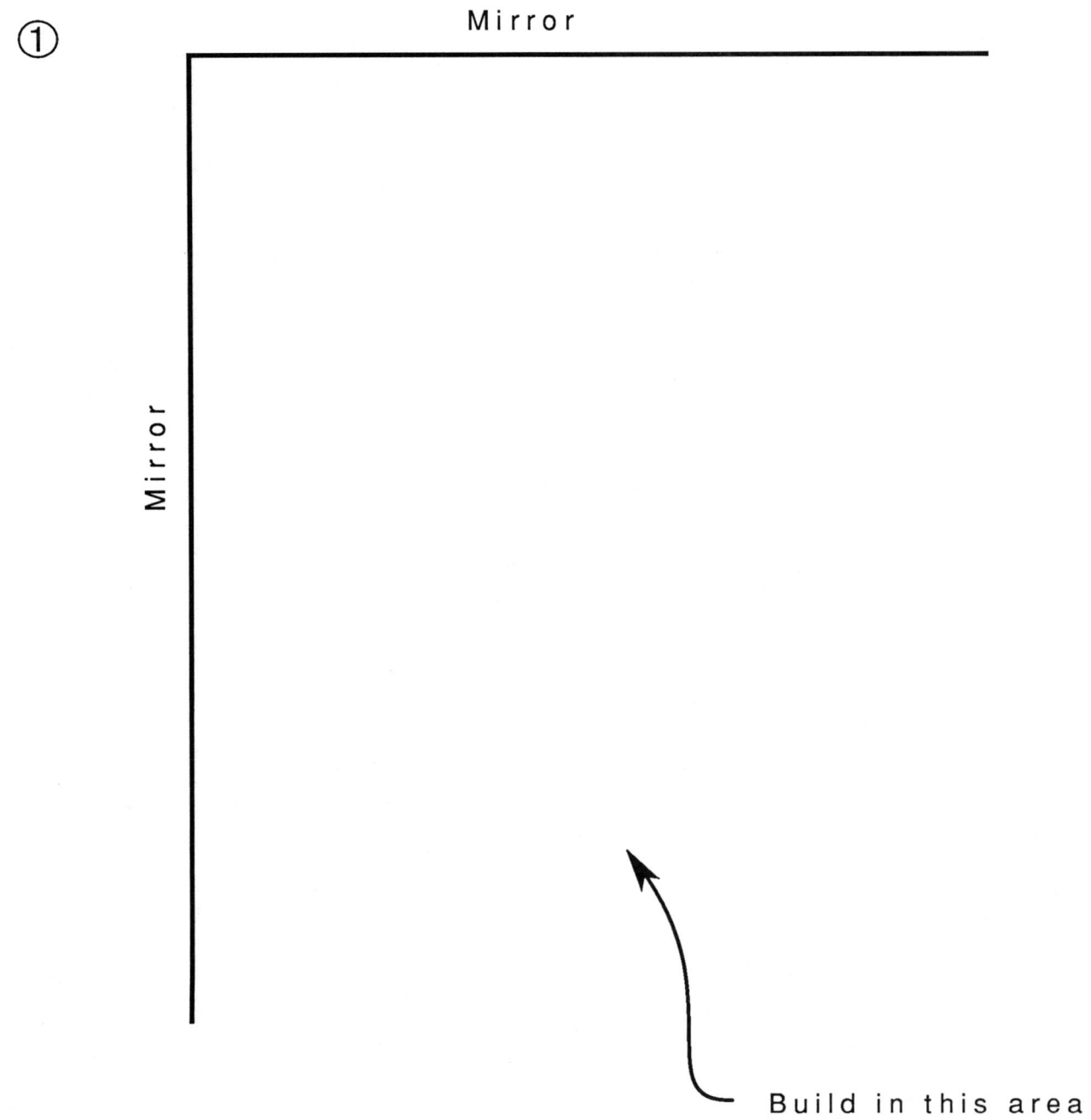

① Mirror / Mirror / Build in this area

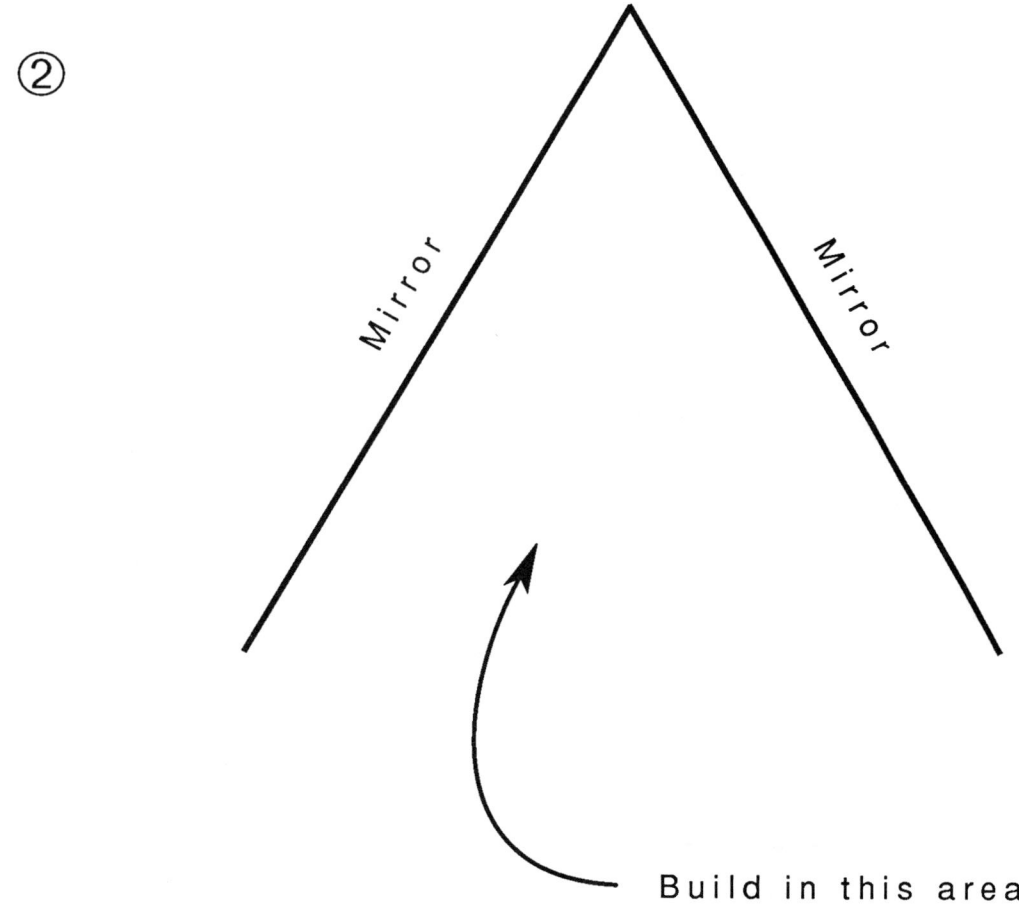
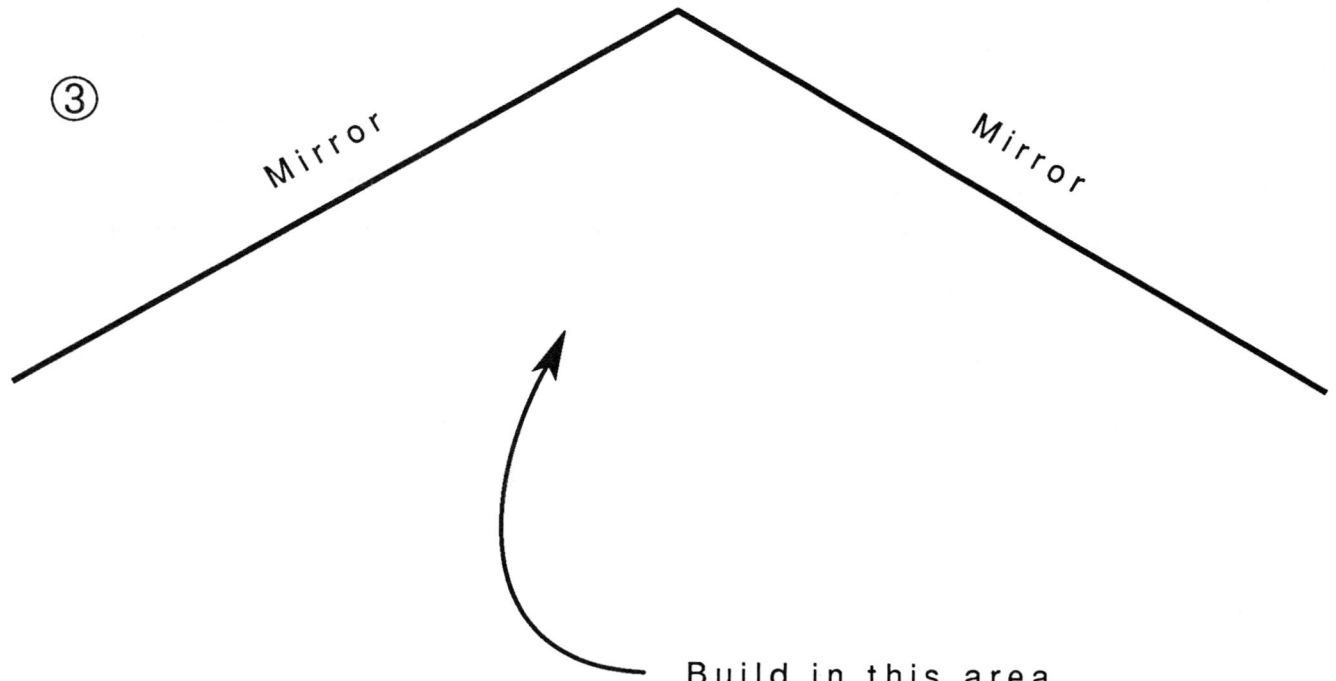

Recording Sheet for Two Mirror Explorations

Use This

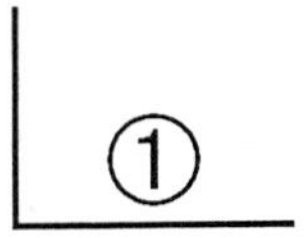

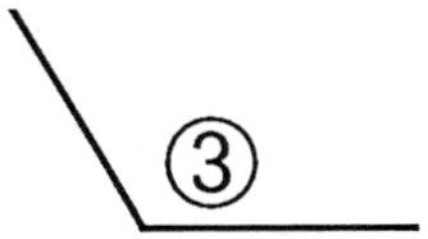

1¢

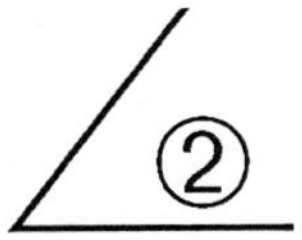

▷

| Draw what you see | ① | ∠② | ∠③ |

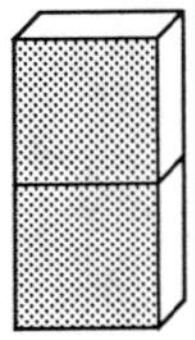

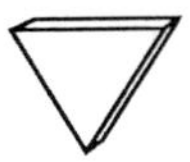

Make a large chart of your discoveries.

Two Mirror Math Challenges

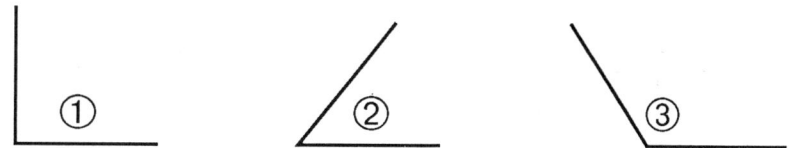

1. 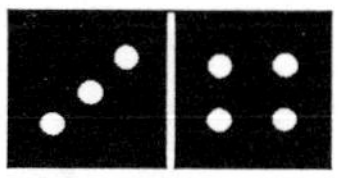    7 x 4 =   7 x ___ =   ___ x ___ =

   7

2.

3.

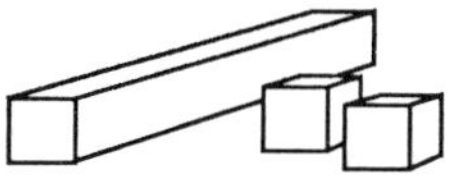

Invent your own!

Two Mirror Investigations

Angles

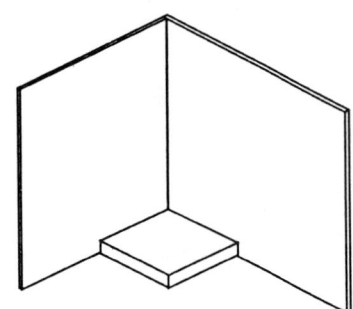

Hinge two mirrors together like this.

Use pattern blocks to make an angle. How many blocks do you see?

Angle	Number of Blocks You See
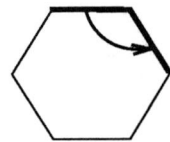	
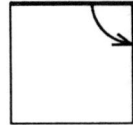	
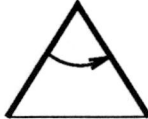	

What rule can you make about this?

There are 360° in a circle.

Draw a dot. Put the corner of a pattern block on the dot.

How many of the same block does it take to go around the dot?

To find the size of the angle, divide 360° by the number of blocks.

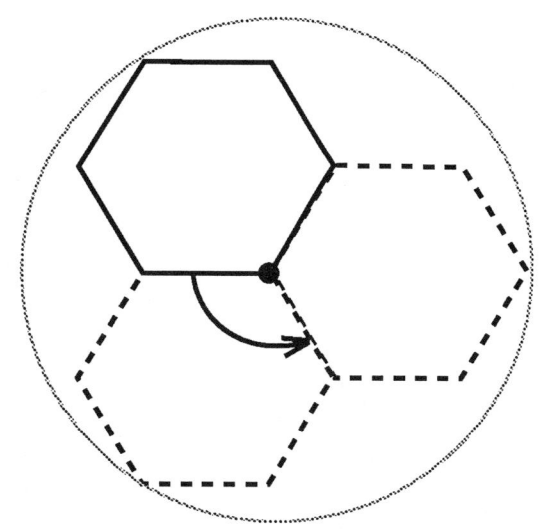

Block Used	Number to Go Around	Problem	Size of Angle
(hexagon)	3	360 ÷ 3 =	
(square)		360 ÷	
(triangle)		360 ÷	
(rhombus)		360 ÷	
(trapezoid)		360 ÷	

Use this method to name the size of other angles found on tangrams, geoblocks, paper triangles or angles that you draw.

Two Mirror Investigations

Finding angles with more than one block.

Blocks Used	Number To Go Around	Problem	Total Size of Angle
(rhombus) and (narrow rhombus)		360° ÷	
(square) (narrow rhombus) (trapezoid)			
(hexagon) (narrow rhombus)			

Invent your own.

24
© 1993 ACTIVITY RESOURCES CO., Inc., P.O. Box 4875, Hayward, Ca 94540

Two Mirror investigations

Hinge two mirrors. Place the hinge on the dot. Change the angle between the mirrors until you see one of the shapes below. Mark the position of the mirrors. Use a different color for each shape.

Use your hinged mirrors on this liine.

Use a different color each time!

	Number of sides	Name of Polygon	Color
△	3	Triangle	
▢	4	(Square)	————
⬠	5	Pentagon	
⬡	6	Hexagon	
⬣	7	Heptagon	
◯	8	* Octagon	
◯	9	* Nonagon	
◯	10	* Decagon	
◯	12	* Dodecagon	

*Tricky!

THREE MIRROR EXPLORATIONS

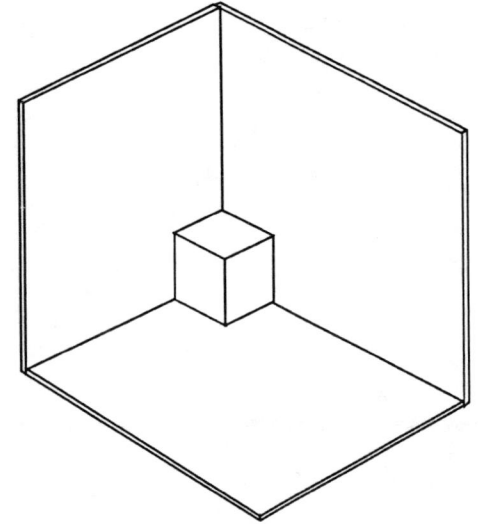

Put one cube
in the corner.
Next to the mirror,
build what you see.

Number of blocks in the mirrors.	Blocks needed to build what you see.
1	
2	
3	
4	
5	
10	

What did you discover? _____

Reflective Challenges

Use three mirrors.

Guess first. Can you build next to the mirror?

Circle Yes or No

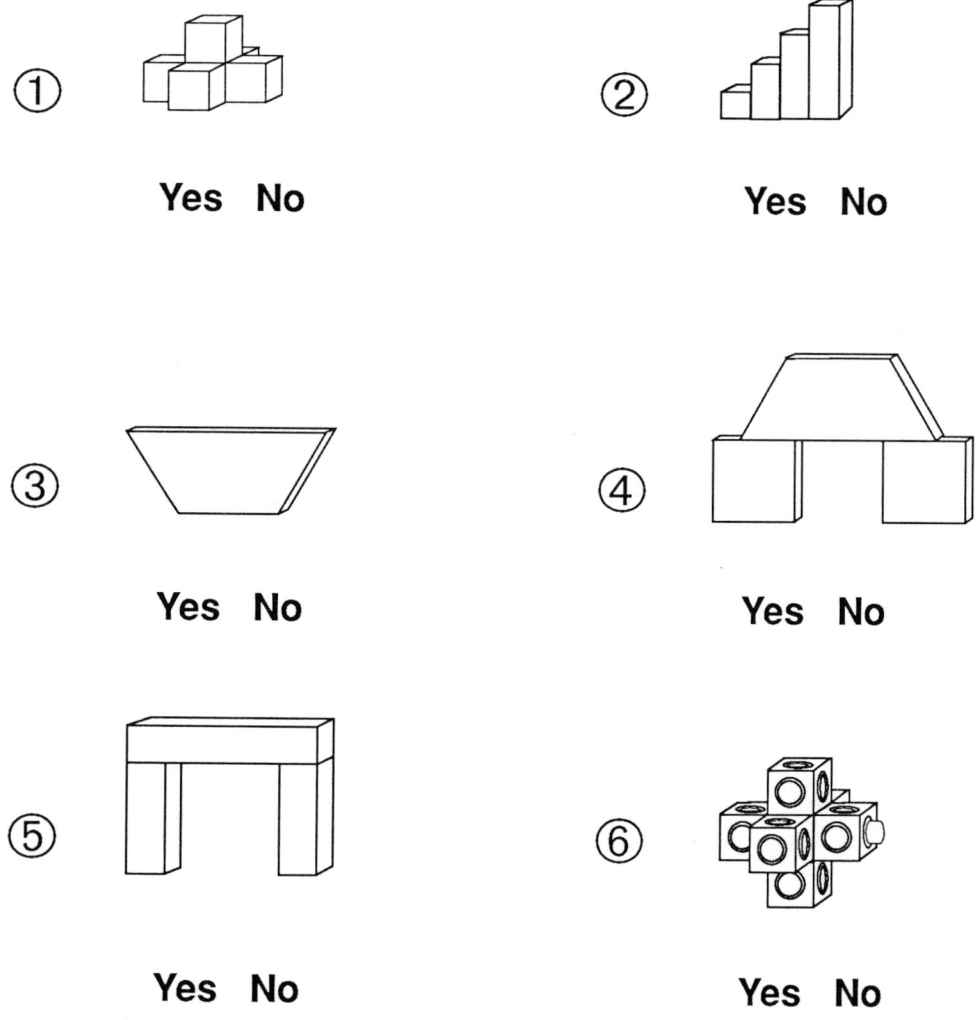

①   Yes   No

②   Yes   No

③   Yes   No

④   Yes   No

⑤   Yes   No

⑥   Yes   No

SYMMETRY

Cut out each shape. How many different ways can you fold each shape in half. Draw each fold line a different color.

Shape Symmetry Recording Sheet

Shape	Sketch	Draw the lines of symmetry. Number of folds = Number of lines of symmetry.
Square	□	4 lines shown (vertical, horizontal, two diagonals)
Isosceles Triangle	△	
Equilateral Triangle	△	
Trapezoid	⏢	
Rectangle	▭	
Circle	○	
Hexagon	⬡	
Parallelogram	▱	
Pentagon	⬠	
Diamond	◇	

Inventing Symmetrical Designs

Use blocks, magazine pictures, trademarks. Build and record.

Check with your mirror.

Make a large mural!

0 lines of symmetry

General Electric Company™

1 line of symmetry

2 lines of symmetry

Keep going!

Pattern Block Symmetry Challenges

Use all blocks each time!

With ▢ ▢ ◿ ◺

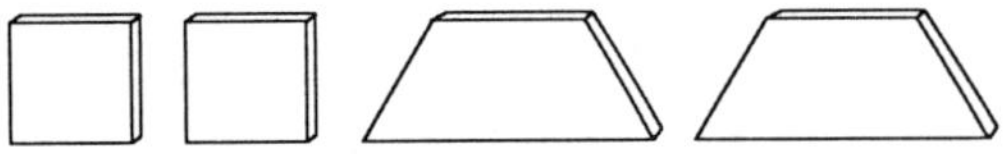

Build a shape with

    0 lines of symmetry

    1 line

    2 lines

Pattern Block Symmetry Challenges

Use all blocks each time!

With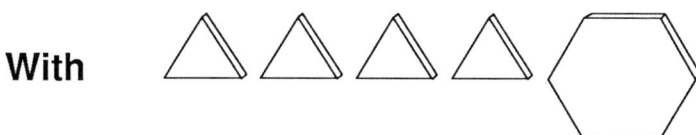

Build and record.

0 lines of symmetry

1 line   **2 lines**

3 lines

Invent your own!

Rod Symmetry Challenges

Use all blocks each time!

With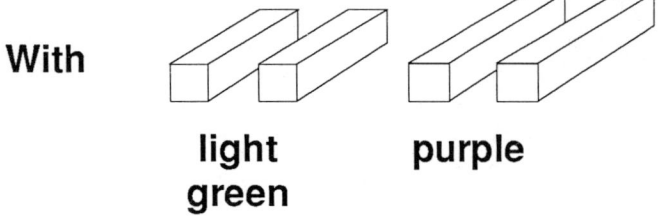

light green   purple

Build and reocrd.

How many ways can you do each one?

0 lines

1 line

2 lines

Rod Symmetry Challenges

Use all blocks each time!

With

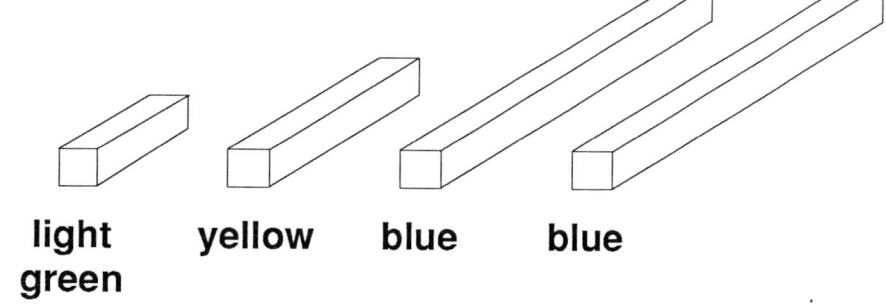

light green yellow blue blue

0 lines

1 line

2 lines

Invent your own!

Colored Squares Symmetry Challenge

This shape has four lines of symmetry.

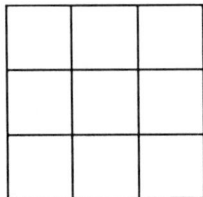

Challenge: Build different squares using only two colors.

How many lines of symmetry does your design have?

Record each solution. Use larger paper to display results.

	Patterns
0 lines	
1 line	
2 lines	
4 lines	

Challenge: Use more than two colors.
          OR
Make larger squares!

(Selected answers on p. 54)

Colored Squares Recording Sheet

Symmetry of Symbols

Symmetry of Numbers and Letters.

What basic shape are they:

How many lines of symmetry do you expect?

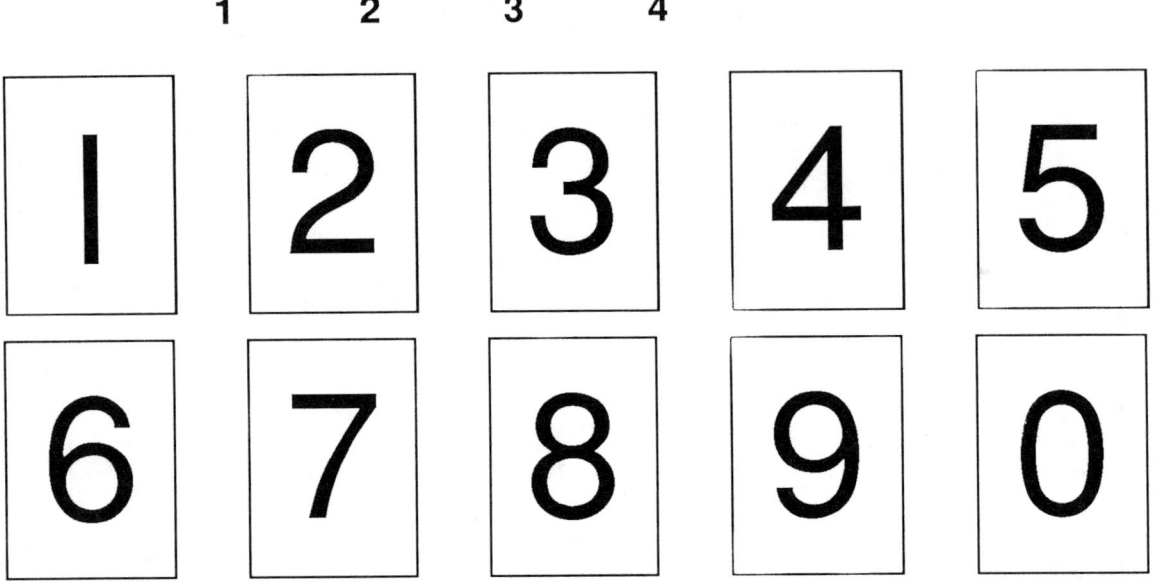

Use your mirror. Draw in the lines of symmetry.

Write some bigger numbers that are symmetric

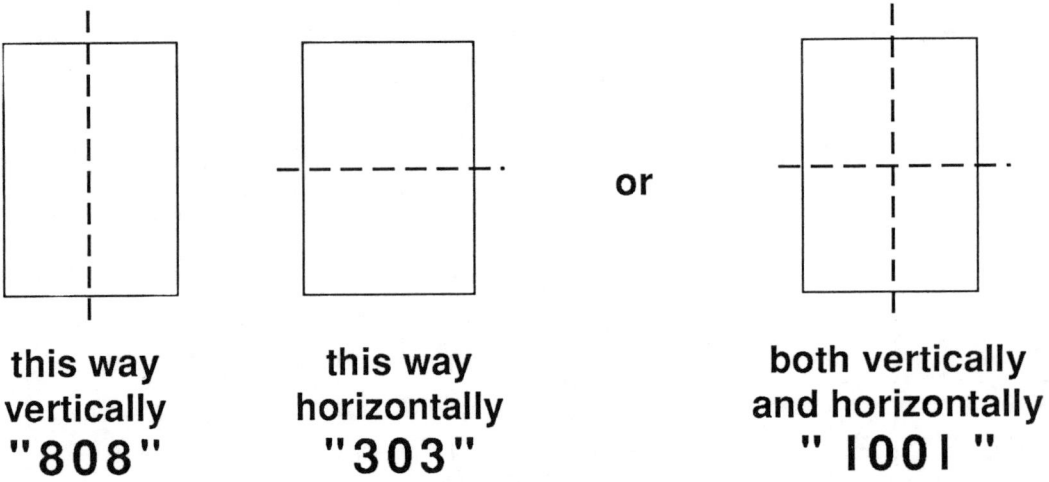

Symmetry of Capital Letters

A B C D E F G H I J K L M N O P Q R S T U V W X Y Z

Which letters have vertical symmetry?

_____ _____ _____ _____

_____ _____ _____ _____

_____ _____ _____

Which letters have horizontal symmetry?

_____ _____ _____

_____ _____ _____

_____ _____ _____

Which letters have both vertical and horizontal?

_____ _____ _____

Word Symmetry Challenge

How many words can you find that have horizontal or vertical symmetry?
Cut out grid paper. Make a large chart

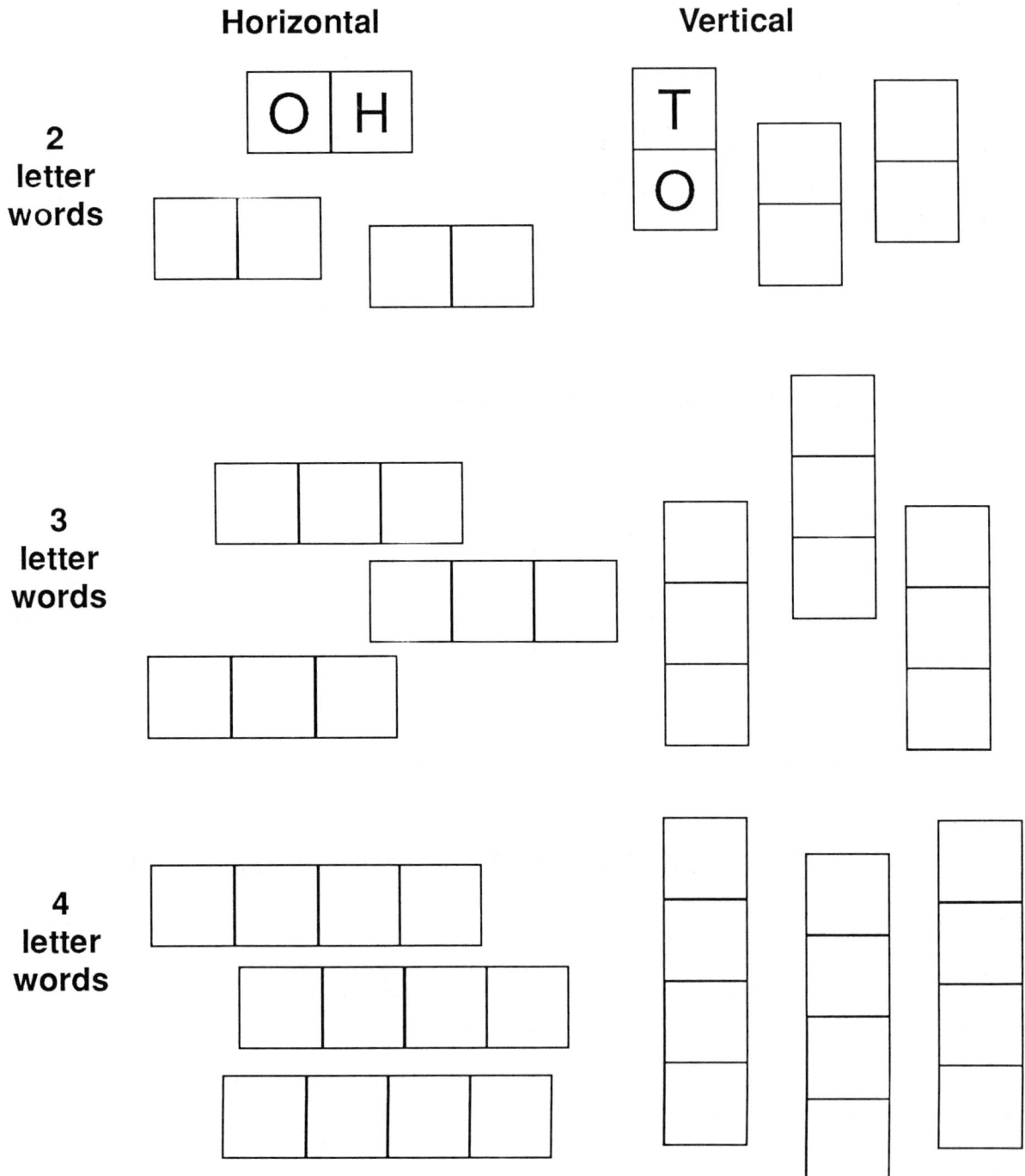

Keep going! Try 5 letter words, 6 letter words . . .

Word Search Symmetry Challenge

Find the words in the puzzle below

K	I	C	K
O	T	O	O
H	I	D	E
I	M	E	X

Vertical Words _____ _____
              _____

Horizontal Words _____ _____
                _____

Hide your own!

Picture Puzzles — Opposites

Messy Bed   **Neat Bed**

Full

Empty

Cracked   New

Invent your own!

Picture Puzzles — More or Less

Counting: How many can you see? Circle the numbers

How many people can you see?

1 2 3 4 5 6 7 8

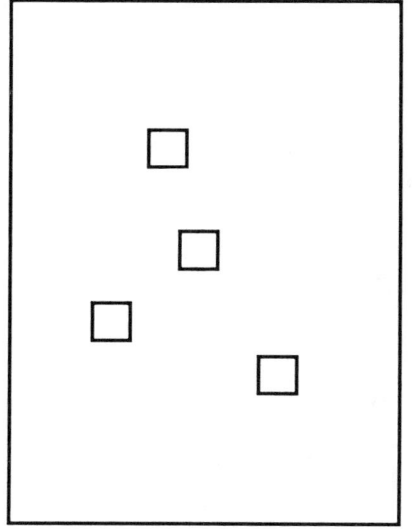

1
2
3
4
5
6
7
8

1
2
3
4
5
6
7
8

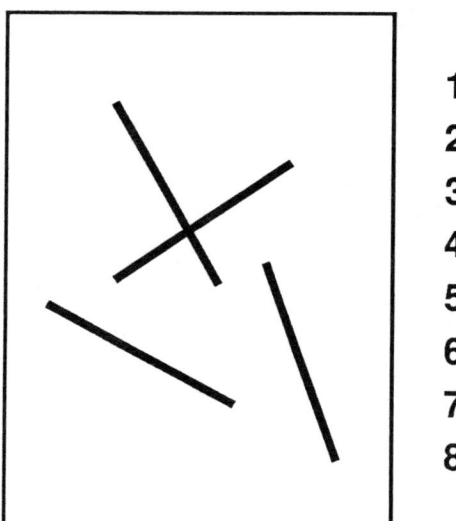

1
2
3
4
5
6
7
8

Invent your own!

Reflective Challenges

Which of the pictures below can make the hot dog?
Can you find them?

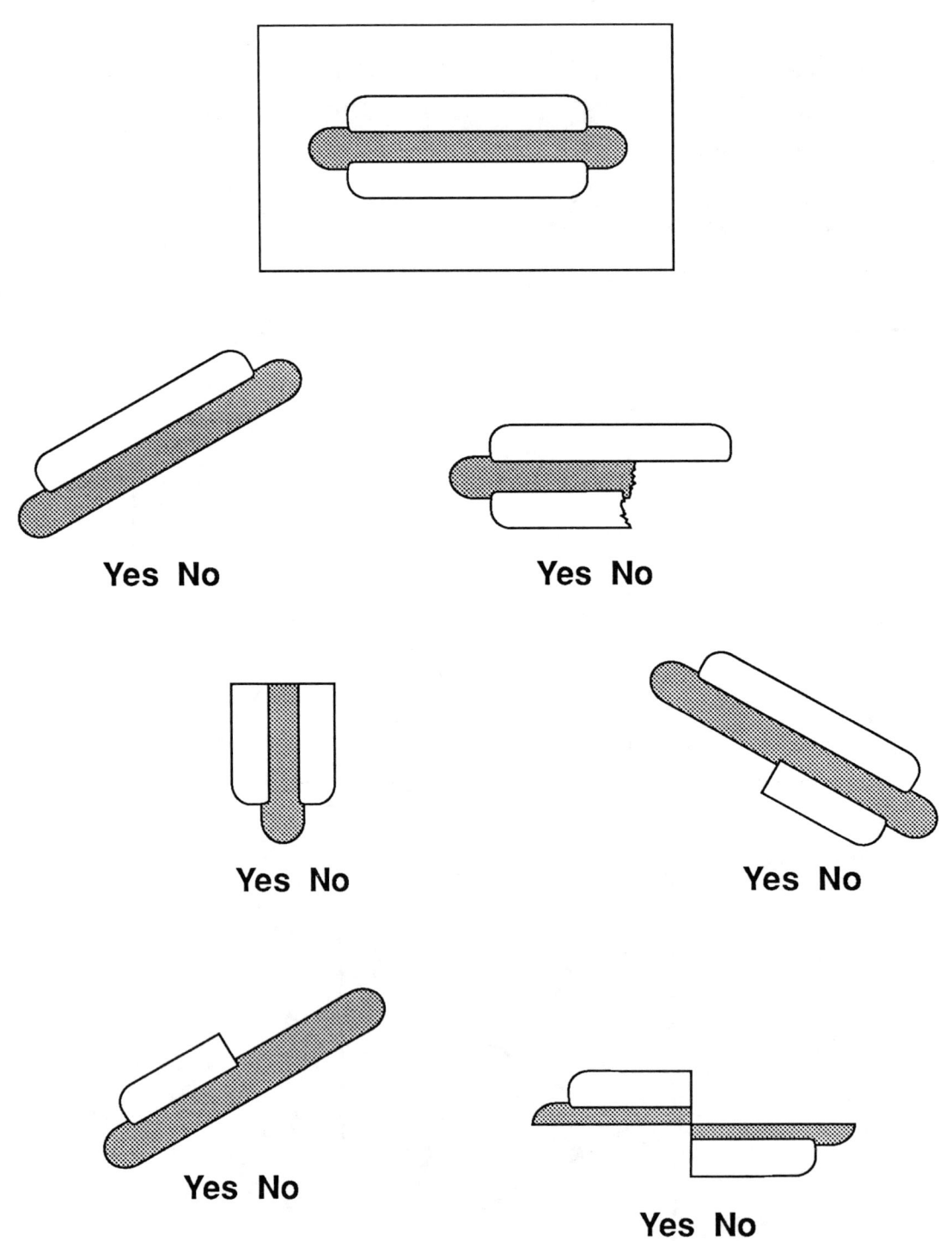

Yes No

Yes No

Yes No

Yes No

Yes No

Yes No

Reflective Challenges

Which of the pictures below make this pattern?
Can you find them?

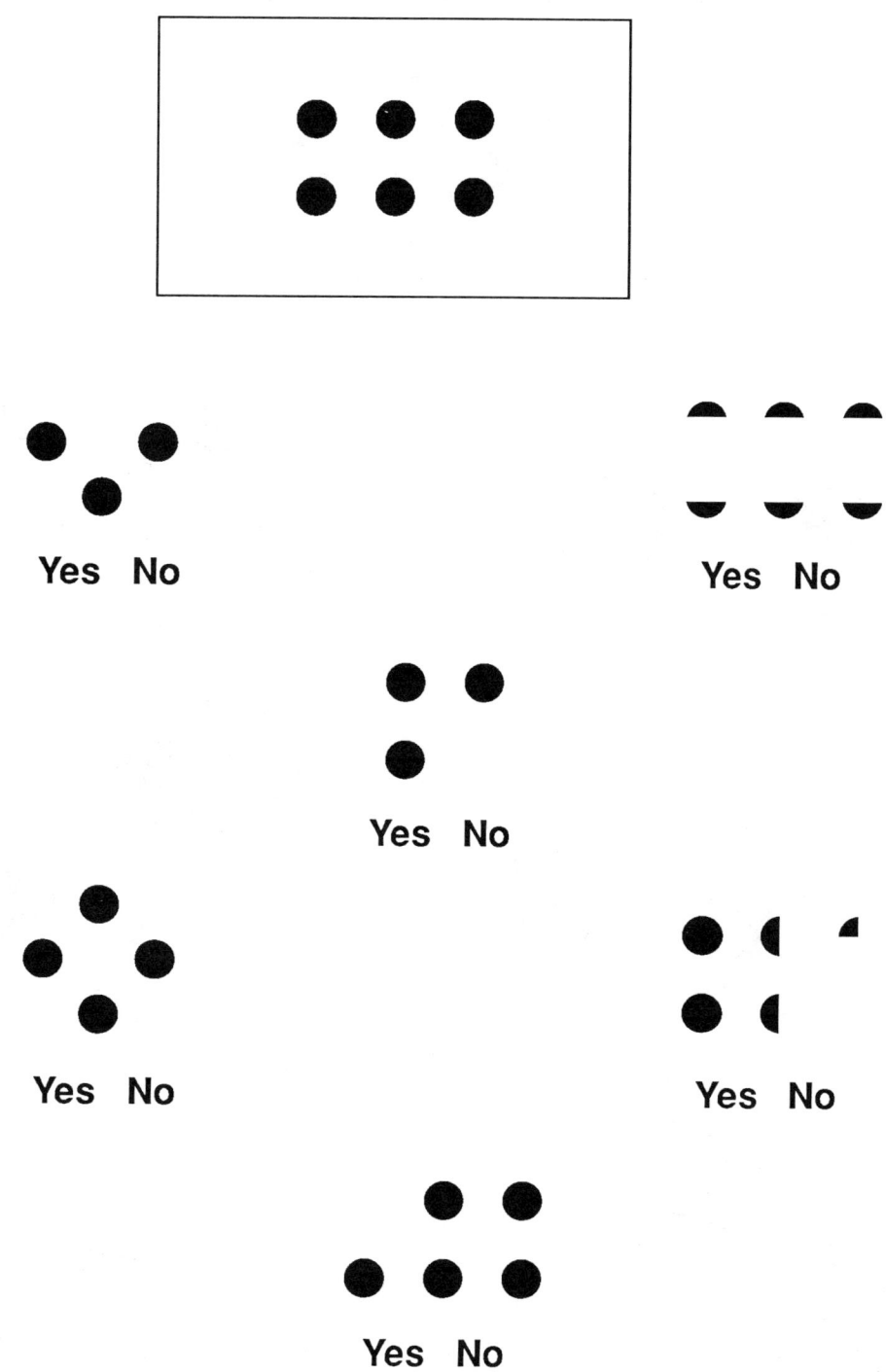

Reflective Challenges

Use the mirror on the picture in the box below to decide which pictures can be made.

Yes   No

Yes   No

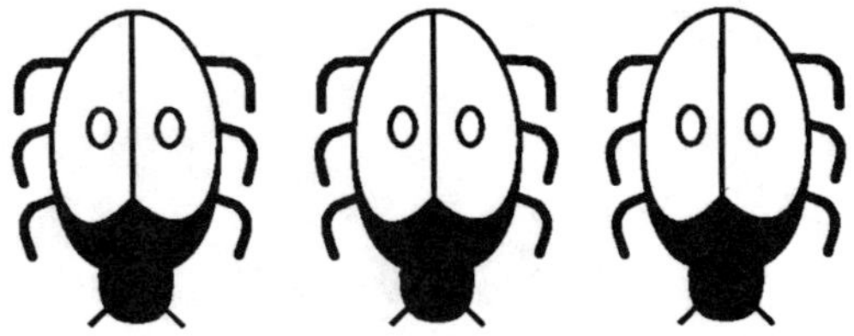

Yes   No

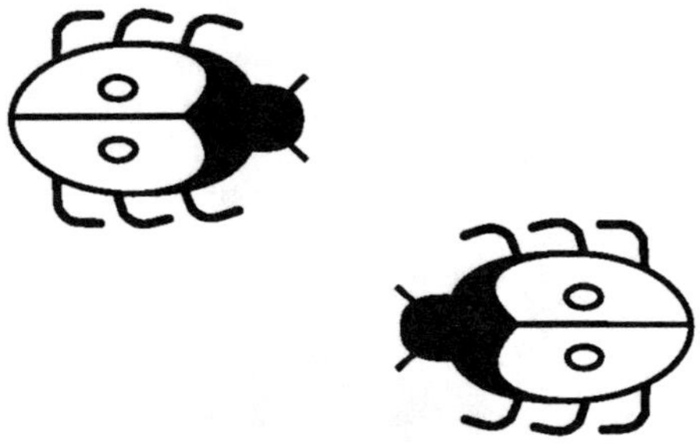

Yes   No

Yes   No

Yes   No

Reflective Challenges

Use the mirror on the picture in the box below to decide which pictures can be made.

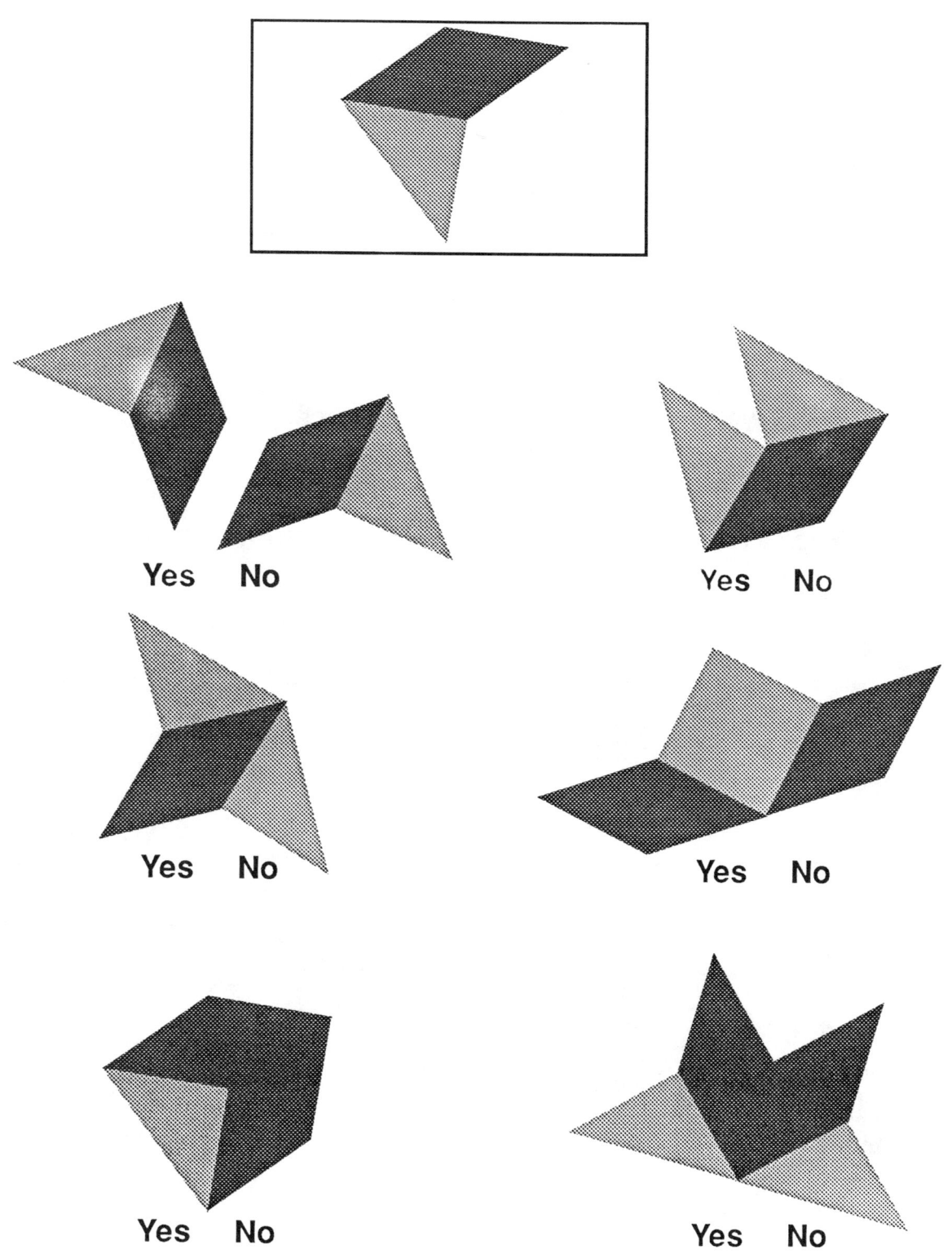

Reflective Challenges

Use the mirror on the picture in the box below to decide which pictures can be made.

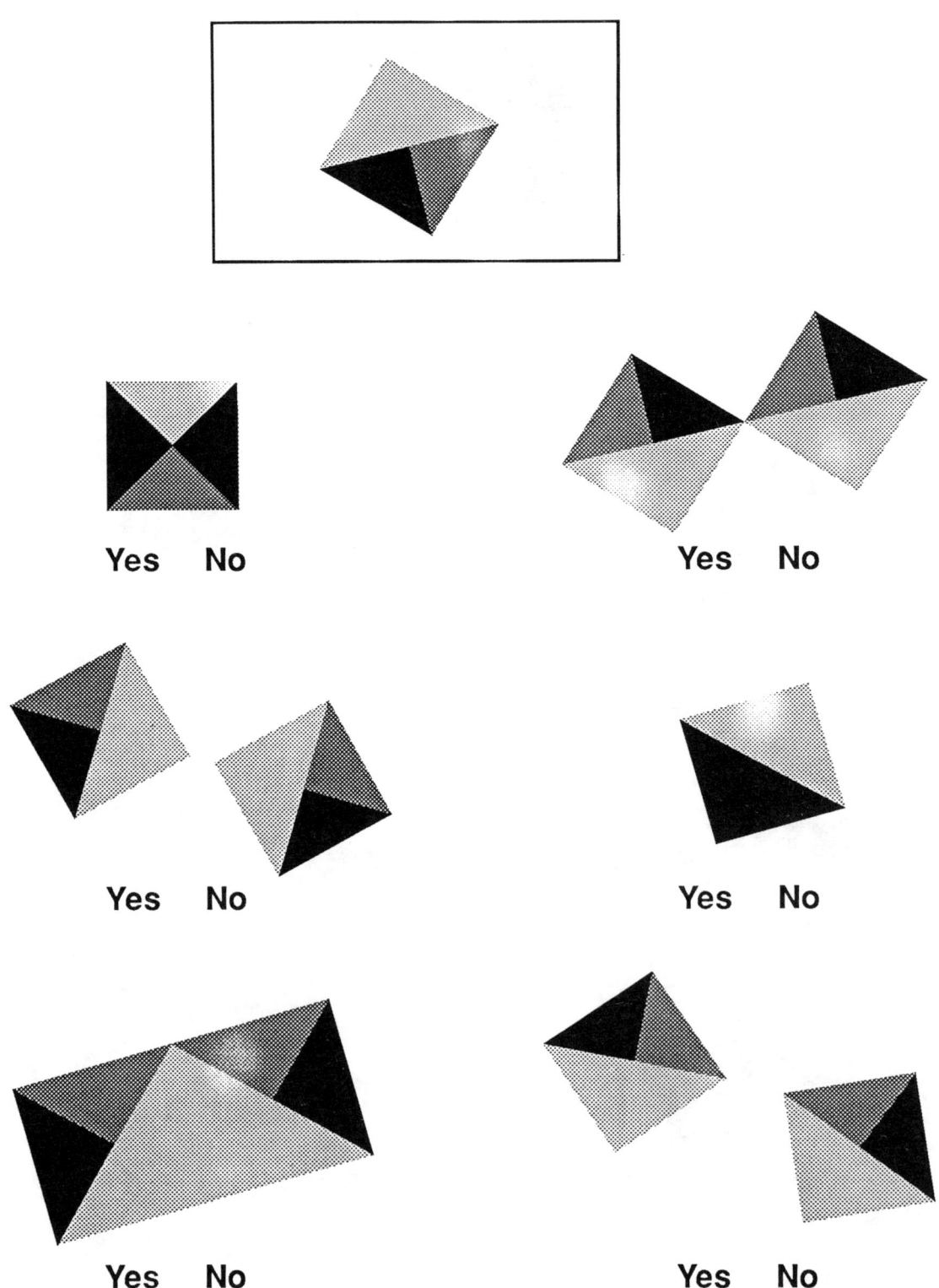

Reflective Challenges

Use the mirror on the picture in the box below to decide which pictures can be made.

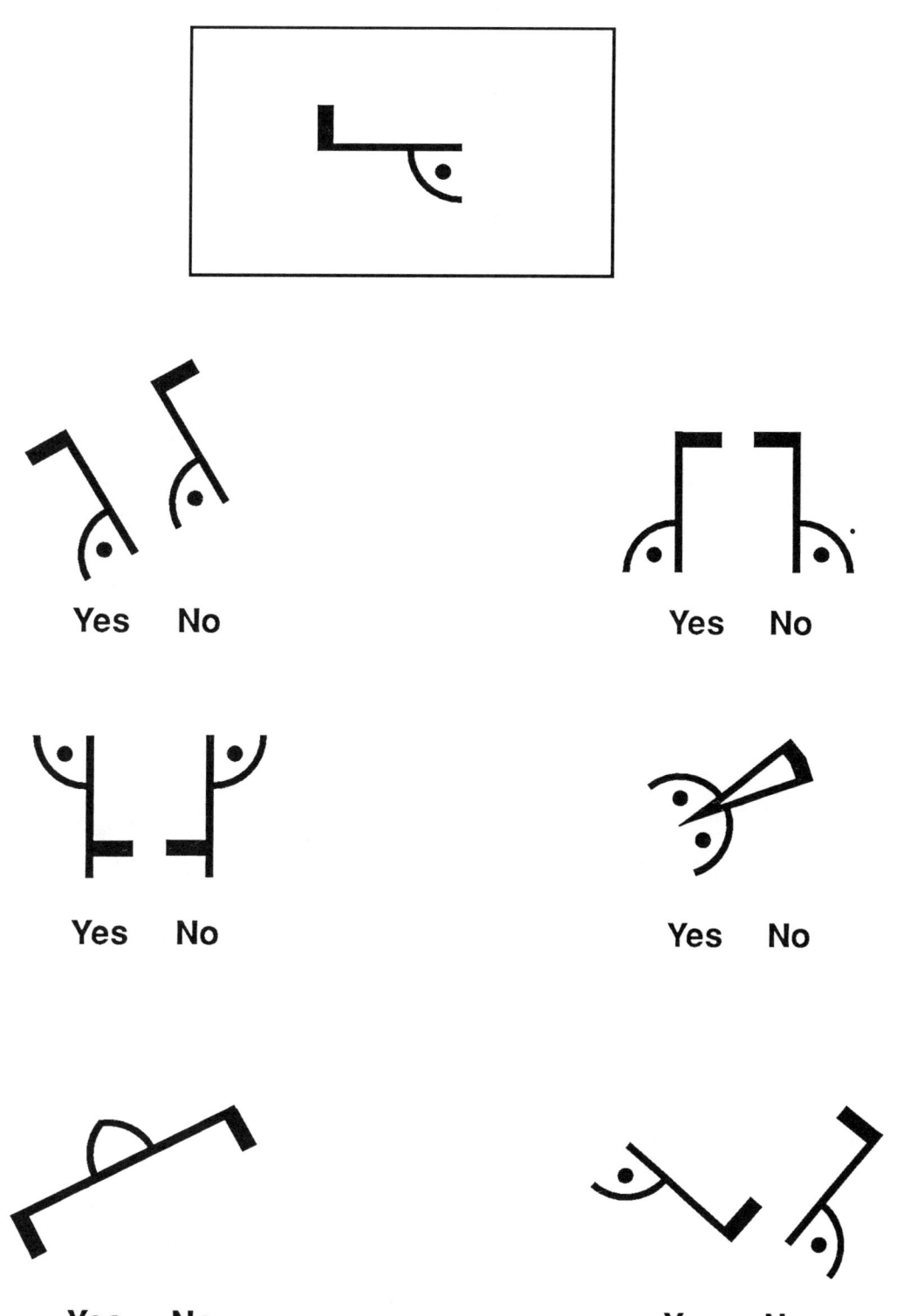

Reflective Challenges

Use the mirror on the picture in the box below to decide which pictures can be made.

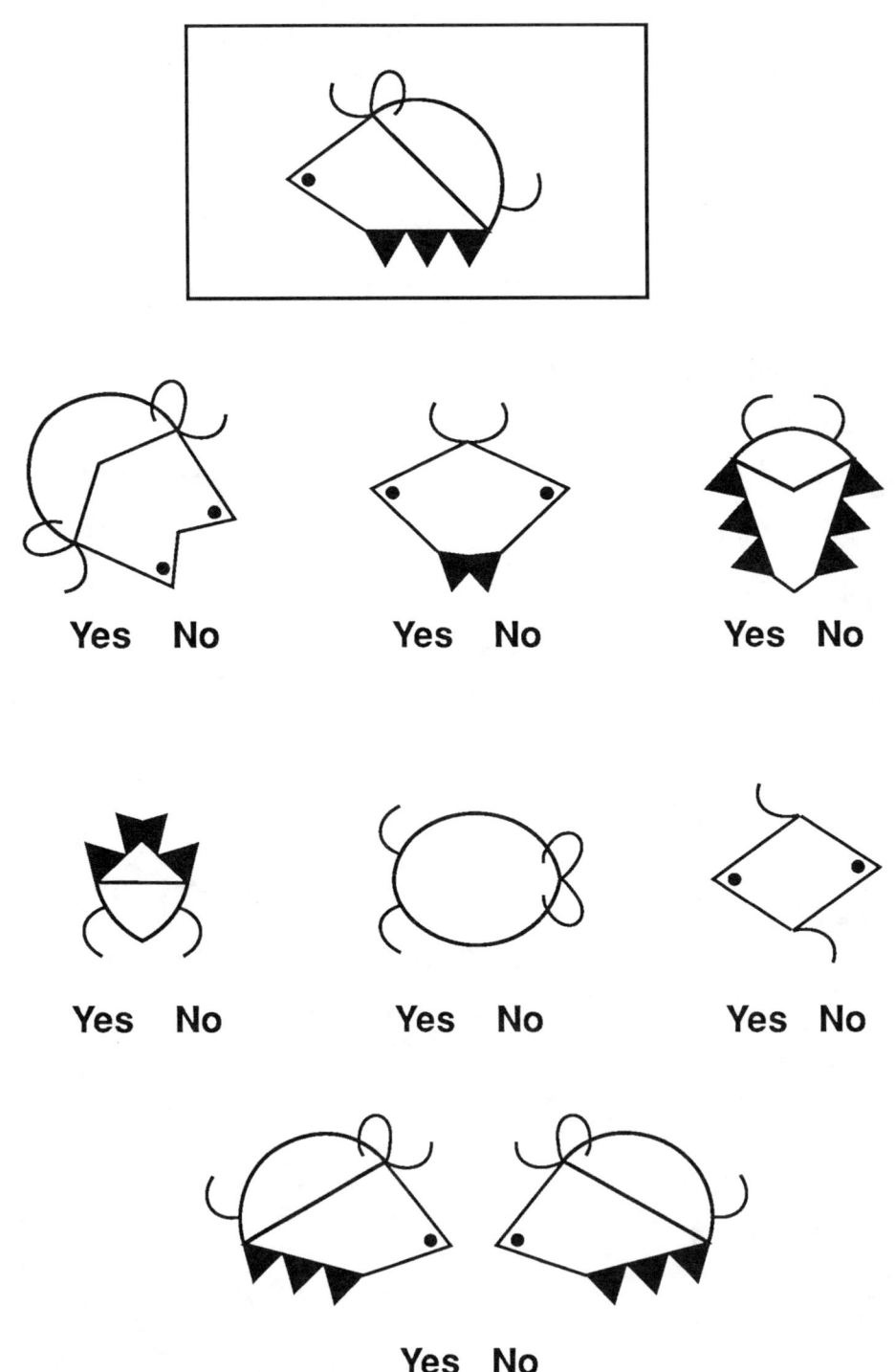

Reflective Challenges

Use the mirror on the picture in the box below to decide which pictures can be made.

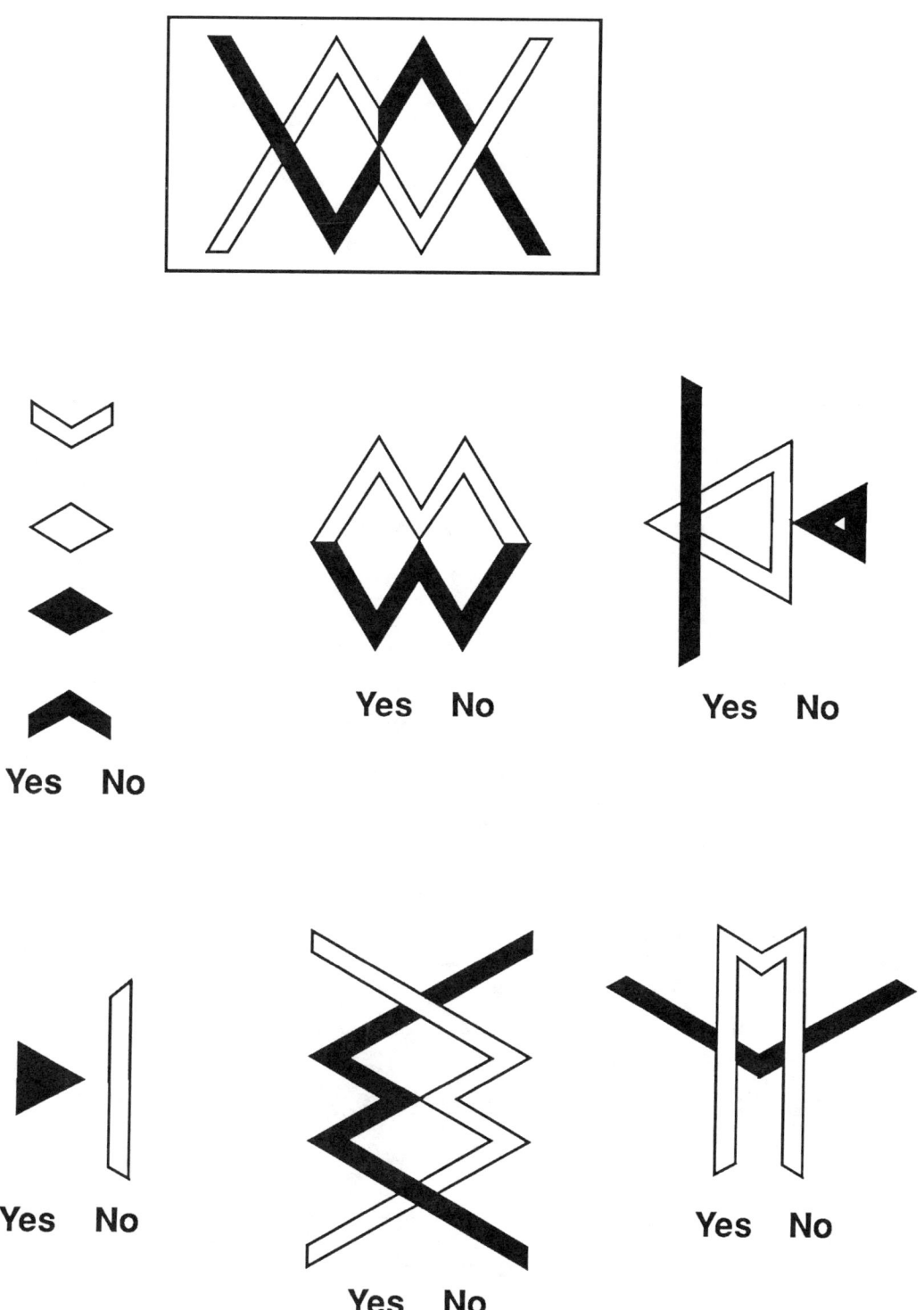

Design Your Own Mirror Puzzles

Start with any object.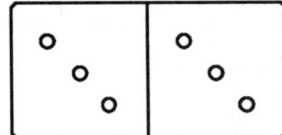

Put the mirror different places to create new objects.

Sketch your results!

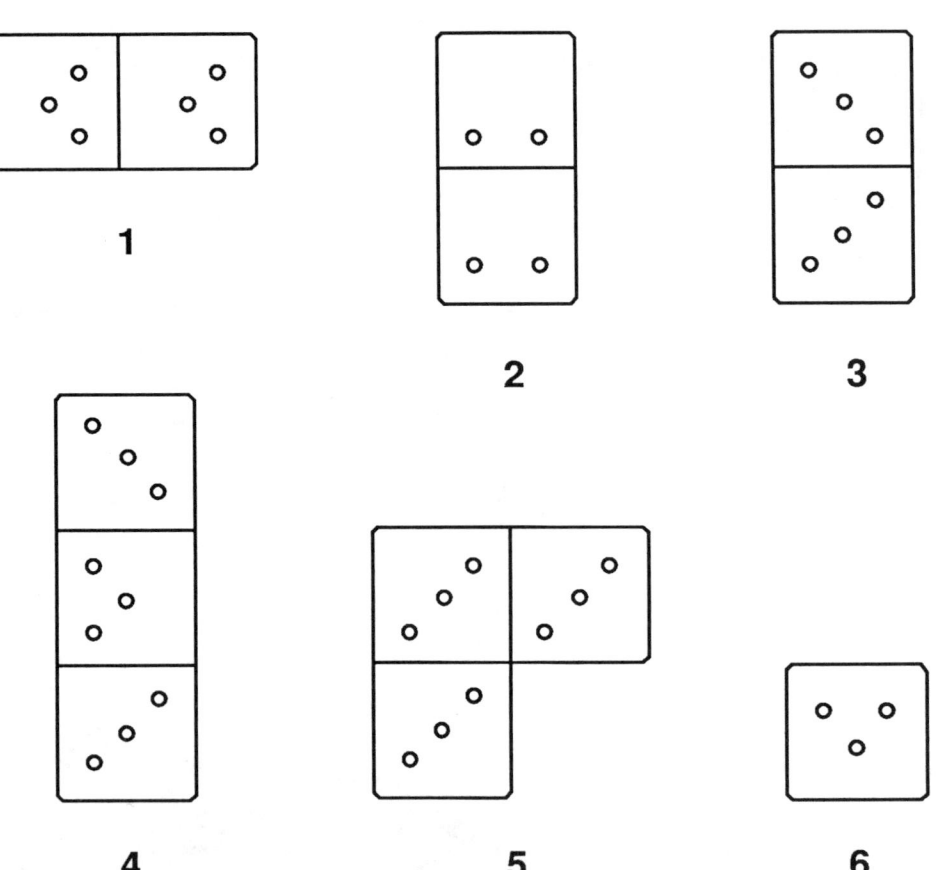

Draw a dotted line on your shape to prove how you did it!

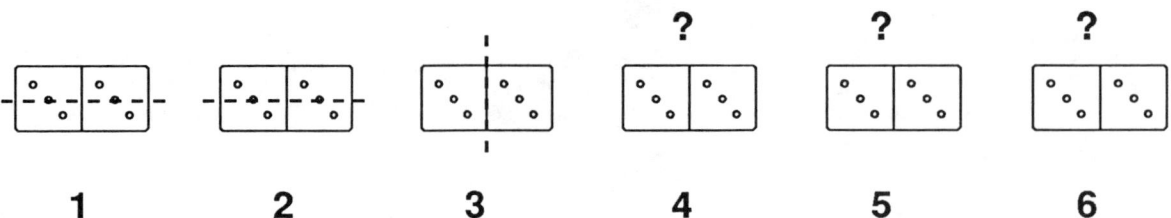

Design Your Own Mirror Puzzles

Cut up this page. Make your own picture puzzles using the beginning shape. Record solutions on numbered figures.

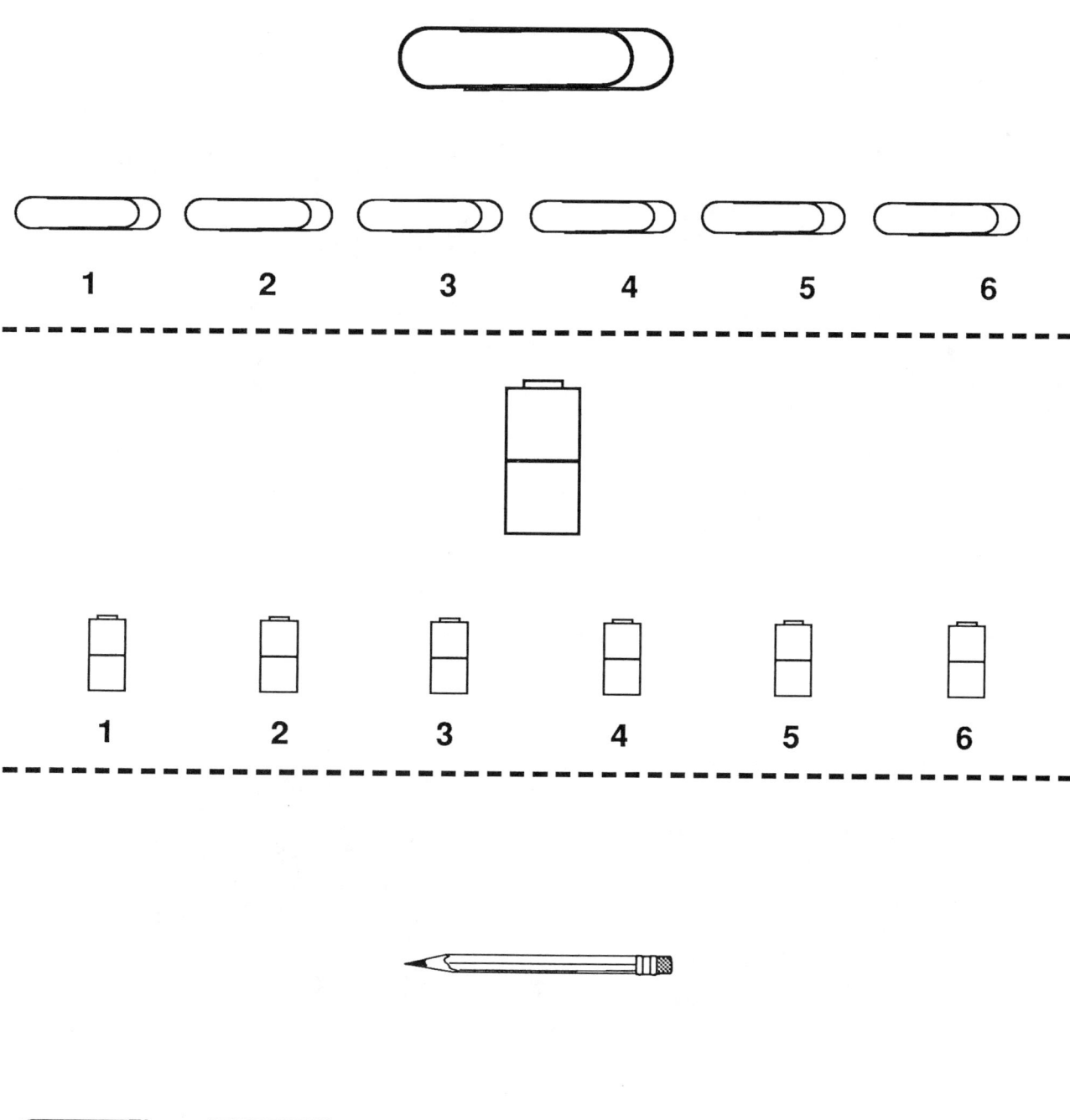

53
© 1993 Activity Resources Co., Inc., P.O. Box 4875, Hayward, Ca 94540

Solutions
Some possible solutions for Colored Squares Symmetry Challenge

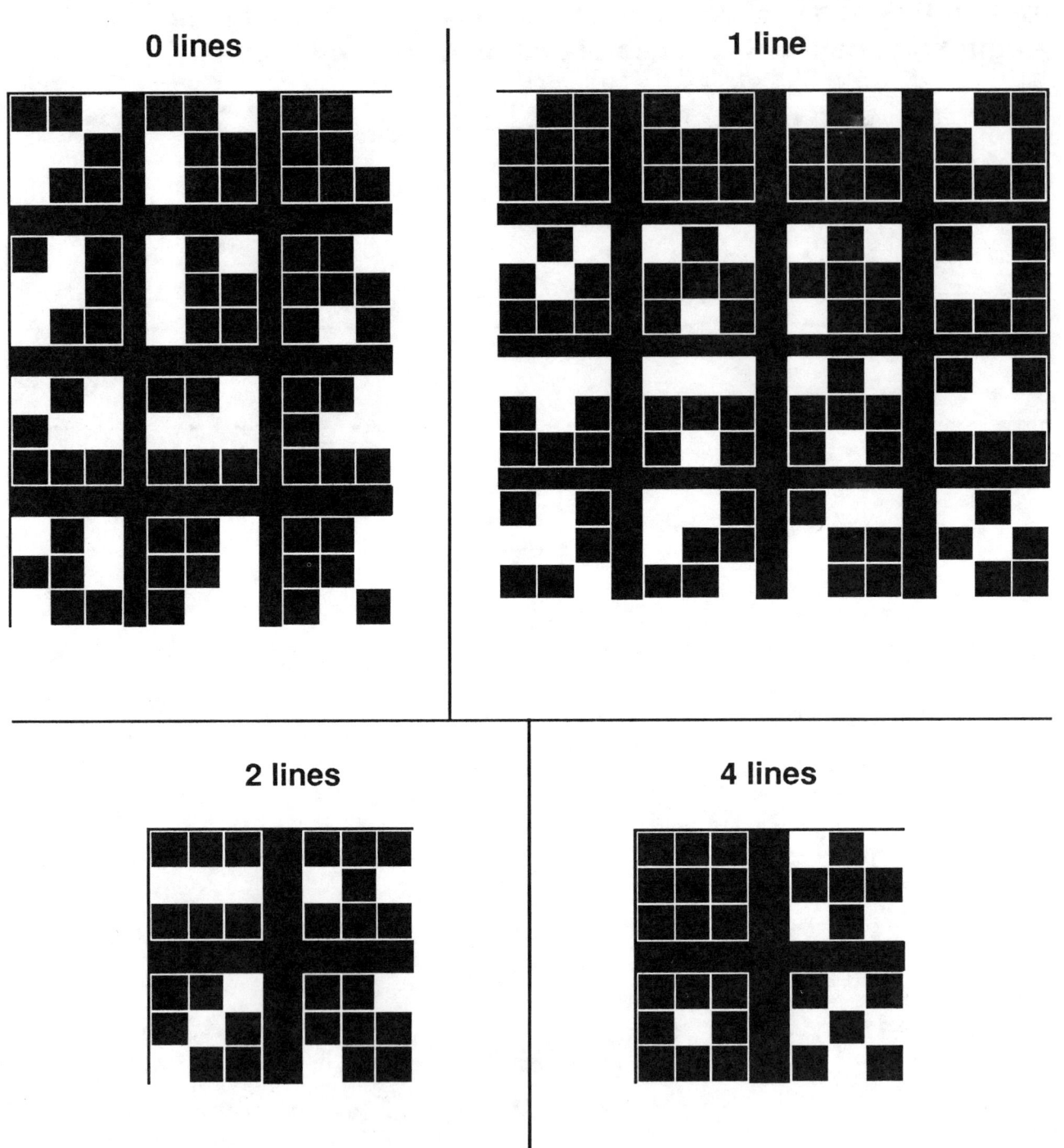

0 lines   **1 line**   **2 lines**   **4 lines**

This puzzle was presented by James K. Bidwell in the March 1987 Arithmetic Teacher